More Praise
Beyond Learning C

"Anyone who has a stake in the success of a project or program—and that is just about everyone in business—needs to read *Beyond Learning Objectives*. Jack and Patti Phillips have written a comprehensive, practical, step-by-step approach to developing measurable objectives. How I wish I had read this guidebook years ago!"

> Patricia M. Crull, PhD
> Vice President and CLO
> Time Warner Cable

"Filled with insights, exercises, and case studies, *Beyond Learning Objectives* clearly demonstrates why every project or program must begin with the right objectives to be successful. This is exactly the information every CEO needs before committing and investing resources."

> Jon Gornstein
> President, Persona Global, Inc.

"Identifying the business objectives supported by learning has not traditionally been a strength of trainers. This book, however, clearly outlines the process of developing business objectives for training in a way that is simple and easy to understand and makes it possible to evaluate a program's success in a credible manner."

> M. Theresa Breining
> President, Concepts Worldwide, Inc.
> Strategic Meeting Management

"In today's competitive global environment, clearly connecting program and project objectives to business results has never been more important. This book will show you exactly how to make this connection and will provide needed support for your bid to participate in strategic decisions at the highest level."

> D. Brian Roulstone
> CEO, Quality Resources

"If you want to show your project's value to the organization with a focus on results, follow the guidelines for developing six different levels of measurable objectives as set out in this book. A great resource to be referred to often as new programs are developed, this book is easy to read, clearly explains the various levels, links the levels forming the chain of impact, and provides numerous tips and exercises throughout."

Madonna Pendley
Senior Director of Finance, RSM McGladrey

"This latest contribution from Jack and Patricia Phillips gives professionals the knowledge and skill to define objectives at multiple levels of evaluation that are clear, complete, specific—and communicate a strong message to stakeholders. It's an excellent practical resource for professionals wanting to maximize the impact of their programs."

John Sherlock
Associate Professor and Director MS Degree in
Human Resources
Western Carolina University

Beyond Learning Objectives

Beyond Learning Objectives:

*Develop Measurable Objectives
That Link to the Bottom Line*

Jack J. Phillips and Patricia Pulliam Phillips

ROI INSTITUTE™

Birmingham, Alabama

Alexandria, Virginia

ASTD Press is an internationally renowned source of insightful and practical information on workplace learning and performance topics, including training basics, evaluation and return-on-investment, instructional systems development, e-learning, leadership, and career development.

Ordering information: Books published by ASTD Press can be purchased by visiting our website at store.astd.org or by calling 800.628.2783 or 703.683.8100.

Library of Congress Control Number: 2007939266

ISBN-10: 1-56286-518-8
ISBN-13: 978-1-56286-518-4

ASTD Press Editorial Staff:
Director: Cat Russo
Manager, Acquisitions and Author Relations: Mark Morrow
Editorial Manager: Jacqueline Edlund-Braun
Senior Associate Editor: Tora Estep
Associate Editor: Maureen Soyars

Copyeditor: Scott Long
Indexer: April Davis
Proofreader: Kris Patenaude
Interior Design and Production: PerfecType, Nashville, TN
Cover Design: Alizah Epstein
Cover Art: Getty Images, www.gettyimages.com

Printed by Victor Graphics, Inc., Baltimore, Maryland, www.victorgraphics.com.

Contents

Preface

Developing measurable objectives is perhaps the most important action that can be undertaken to ensure that projects or programs focus on results. This is a fundamental concept taught in our workshops, where we have trained more than 20,000 people in the implementation of the ROI Methodology. Moving beyond the classic development of learning objectives designed for most projects or programs, this new book, *Beyond Learning Objectives: Develop Measurable Objectives That Link to the Bottom Line*, shows step-by-step how to develop input, reaction, learning, application, impact, and even ROI objectives. Anyone developing a new project or program designed to drive performance improvement and business impact will find the exercises, tips, guidelines, and examples included in the book not only easy to use, but also an essential reference.

The Need for This Book

Walk into any learning and development department and you can quickly see the progress made in developing learning objectives. Trainers, learning specialists, development coordinators, performance improvement analysts, and many others have made tremendous strides in developing effective learning objectives. Why? In the 1960s, Robert Mager brought the issue of objectives clearly into focus with his book *Preparing Instructional Objectives*. Through many reprints and editions, this 62-page book has been a classic in the learning and development, education, and performance improvement fields. By showing how to develop meaningful, specific learning objectives, Mager helped professionals understand how to develop focused content supporting these specific objectives. Many would agree that Mager's influence is represented in the current progress in developing excellent learning objectives. His classic work has sold more than 1.5 million copies. Mager is no longer active in this field, but the book remains a classic, and professionals around the world recognize his name and his contribution.

Since that book was published, the need for evaluation data has changed. Data beyond what participants learn are needed to ensure that programs are working and showing value. To provide these data, programs and projects must be developed to achieve the results sought—this requires levels of objectives historically ignored. While there is a need for continuing focus on improving learning objectives, application and impact objectives must be developed to provide focus and direction to key stakeholders. Also, there is a legitimate need for input and reaction objectives, and even ROI objectives. Add to this the growing need for more detailed objectives in human resources, technology, quality, and marketing, and it's obvious that a new book about developing objectives has a deliberate purpose.

Mager once said, "We should never develop objectives that we cannot control. We develop learning objectives only because we can control them in a classroom." Now, even Mager would agree: Higher levels of objectives (particularly at the application and impact levels) provide focus for the participant, the facilitator, the designer, the developer, and the evaluator.

Mager was right—facilitators do not have complete control of objectives beyond the classroom. However, they can influence and ensure that facilitation positions participants for successful application. Objectives are developed for all stakeholders of the program. The facilitator has more control over the success of learning objectives, but the participants have more control over the success of application and impact objectives. The participants' manager also influences the success of application and impact objectives. Program sponsors have more control over input and ROI objectives. Program designers have more control over the success of reaction objectives. Evaluators need all of the objectives so they know how to measure program success. You get the picture. Because many stakeholders must make these objectives work, different levels of objectives are needed to drive results.

Professionals in learning and development, education, performance improvement, technology, quality, and marketing need tools that will ensure initial business alignment keeps projects and programs focused on results. At the same time, they need to simplify the design, development, delivery, and evaluation of projects or programs. Clearly defined objectives provide help with all of these issues. Analysts develop these objectives directly from a needs assessment.

Designers and developers need clear direction as they develop content with specific examples, exercises, skill practices, and other processes to achieve success on the job. Facilitators and program organizers need clear direction on how to prepare individuals to implement the program and use the skills.

Participants need guidance about what they should achieve as a result of participating in a program or project. Objectives allow them to see clearly and understand the expectations and desired outcomes. Those who support or fund projects and programs need assurances that the program will add value beyond learning. Higher levels of objectives provide the connection to results. Some executives suggest, "It is not what they learn, but what they do with what they learn that makes the difference." Evaluators struggling to measure the impact of a variety of different programs need all the help they can get. All levels of objectives tell them when, what, and how to measure the success when the objective is met.

In summary, this book will be a valuable guide to help all professionals involved in implementing projects, programs, initiatives, and solutions. It is a valuable, essential guide for the performance improvement communities. It will help managers, analysts, designers, developers, project leaders, facilitators, participants, sponsors, and evaluators increase the effectiveness of their work by creating clearly focused objectives that are perfectly aligned to their businesses.

How to Use This Book

This book describes a logical process and should be read sequentially. After the first read through, each part will serve as a quick reference as the reader begins to apply the content. The following tips focus on the frequently asked questions about developing objectives and provide readers with a guide to help find more detail on each issue.

Use this book when you need to do the following:

> **Convince others about the value and power of objectives.** This issue is crucial when asking stakeholders to develop objectives. They must see the value in objectives. This material is covered in detail in chapter 1, as the reasons for developing objectives are highlighted. However, subsequent chapters on the different levels of objectives offer clues as to the power of objectives.

> **Know when to develop objectives.** An obvious question is, when should objectives be developed? Chapter 2 shows why it is important to develop them at the beginning of a project. The case study in chapter 9 shows

that objectives can be developed in meetings with stakeholders even after the initial needs assessment is completed.

> **Determine who should develop objectives.** Chapter 2 describes the ideal source of objectives. The same chapter shows that others may be involved in helping set the objectives.

> **Know how to develop input and reaction objectives.** Sometimes professionals skip input and reaction objectives, thinking that input is required by the initial request or contract and that a positive reaction is always needed so there is no need to make a formal declaration. However, the project parameters should be clearly defined with input objectives. Chapter 3 provides the detail. The desired reaction from participants is critical. Chapter 4 shows how reaction objectives are developed.

> **Know how to develop learning objectives.** This may not be a concern for some professionals, particularly in the learning and development field, as they have been developing learning objectives for years. However, for a refresher on the basics, chapter 5 provides a quick reference.

> **Know how to develop application objectives.** For some reason, application objectives are often overlooked, assumed, or are not completely developed. These objectives are important. Details on how to develop them are contained in chapter 6.

> **Know how to develop impact objectives.** For some projects, the business connection is clearly known, because these measures often drive the need for the project. In others, the desired business impact is not so clear. Impact objectives are the most powerful set of objectives when linking programs and projects to the business. Chapter 7 explains how to develop them.

> **Know how to develop ROI objectives.** Developing ROI objectives is straightforward. However, the desired percentage return or benefit-cost ratio is often a mystery. Chapter 8 shows the four strategies to set this objective, along with examples.

> **See examples of objectives.** Examples of measures and objectives are provided at the end of most chapters.

> **Practice with objectives.** At the end of each chapter is a simple set of exercises to clarify misunderstandings about objectives. The answers are provided for clarification in Appendix A. Also, Appendix B contains a practical exercise on matching levels with objectives.

> **Experience the dialogue when developing objectives.** A case study in chapter 9 shows the dialogue involved in developing objectives when they were not developed initially by the analyst who determined if the project or program was needed.

> ➤ **See how objectives are a part of a major program.** Many chapters give an example of objectives for a particular program, all intended to show the power and importance of different levels of objectives.
> ➤ **Participate in a special learning opportunity.** For some readers, the best way to learn more about setting objectives is to participate in a workshop where there is an opportunity to learn, explore, and practice with other colleagues. These workshops are available through ASTD and the ROI Institute. Appendix C describes a specific workshop that supports this book.

Acknowledgments

No book is the work of the author alone. Many individuals, groups, and organizations have shaped the development of this work. We learn from our clients, from the participants in our workshops, and from our colleagues in this field. We owe particular thanks to the hundreds of clients with whom we've had the pleasure to work over the past two decades. They have helped develop, mold, and refine the ideas presented in these pages. Most of the objectives listed in this book are based on actual examples used by our client organizations, providing readers with a glimpse of what we find is actually happening.

We're particularly indebted to ASTD and are proud of our partnership with this outstanding organization. This is our 34th book with ASTD and one about which we are most excited. We appreciate the helpful efforts of Mark Morrow, manager of acquisitions and author relations, and Cat Russo, director of ASTD Press—outstanding professionals who make our work pleasurable. Thanks to the production and editorial staff, as well as the marketing staff, for making this book understandable, attractive, and affordable.

Within the ROI Institute, thanks go to our publishing and editorial team. Michelle Segrest, our publishing manager, kept us on track during the development of the manuscript. Special thanks go to Rebecca Benton, our managing editor, for doing a great job producing the final manuscript. And finally, we'd like to thank Karen Wright, our newest addition to the team, for jumping in during the final stages of the editing process.

A special note from Jack: I owe the success of this effort to my wife, Patti, who is my partner, friend, and colleague in this and many other endeavors. Patti is an excellent consultant, an outstanding facilitator, a tenacious researcher, and a talented writer. Her contribution to this book is immeasurable.

A special note from Patti: As always, much love and appreciation go to Jack. You've worked hard to get where you are. Thank you for all you do for me, as well as for others.

Jack J. Phillips
Patricia Pulliam Phillips
September 2008

CHAPTER 1

Why Bother?
The Importance of Objectives

Although the need for program objectives might seem obvious, their value and role are much broader than most people think. In this chapter, we cover why we need specific, measurable program objectives categorized at different levels. More important, we examine the benefits of objectives from many perspectives.

FUNDAMENTAL ISSUES

Before describing the benefits of objectives, a few basic concepts should be addressed. These concepts will set the stage for the remainder of the chapter.

Definition of Objectives

Objectives as described in this book are defined based on research, application, and practice. They are logical, credible, and sequential. An objective is a statement describing an intended outcome rather than a process. It describes one of the key intents of the project or program. Objectives rest on a foundation of important principles.

Levels of objectives. There are six levels of objectives (input, reaction, learning, application, impact, and ROI), as described in Table 1.1. Each level produces an additional category of data, representing different definitions of value. Data are sometimes considered more valuable at the higher levels—by a senior executive, for example. This perspective, however, should not discount the importance of data generated at lower levels, which represent value to other stakeholders, such as facilitators who value reaction data or supervisors who value application data. Program objectives should reflect measures of value important to all stakeholders.

Table 1.1: Levels of Objectives

Level of Objectives	Measurement Focus	Typical Measures
0 — Inputs and Indicators	The input into the project in terms of scope, volume, efficiencies, costs	Participants Hours Costs Timing
1 — Reaction and Perceived Value	Reaction to the project or program, including the perceived value	Relevance Importance Usefulness Appropriateness Intent to use Motivation to take action
2 — Learning and Confidence	Learning to use the content and materials, including the confidence to use what was learned	Skills Knowledge Capacity Competencies Confidence Contacts

3 — Application and Implementation	Use of content and materials in the work environment, including progress with action items and implementation	Extent of use Task completion Frequency of use Actions completed Success with use Barriers to use Enablers to use
4 — Impact and Consequences	The consequences of the use of the content and materials expressed as business impact measures	Productivity Revenue Quality Time Efficiency Customer satisfaction Employee engagement
5 — ROI	Comparison of monetary benefits from program to program costs	Benefit-cost ratio (BCR) ROI (%) Payback period

Chain of impact. For a project or program to add value and result in a positive ROI, a multilevel chain of impact must occur. The program is initiated and participants are involved (Level 0 objectives are met). Participants react to the program in a desired way (Level 1 objectives are met). They acquire skills and knowledge associated with the program (Level 2 objectives are met). They apply what they learned in a variety of ways (Level 3 objectives are met). They realize a positive consequence in the work unit or individual performance area (Level 4 objectives are met). Project leaders determine whether the program benefits exceed the costs at an acceptable rate of return, reflecting the desired ROI (Level 5 objectives are met). For the ROI to be positive, the chain of impact must exist and remain intact.

Conditions. An objective might rest on a certain condition. For example, a participant might be able to use particular software, given a variety of operational situations. Performance is described based on that condition. An objective might be written as: "When a customer becomes angry, the following five steps will be taken." The condition for performance is the customer's behavior.

Criterion. Objectives need to be specific, defining precise amounts, such as "5 percent sales increase" or "95 percent of action items are complete." Most objectives are time based. Application and impact objectives, for example, set deadlines for actions to be completed and impact measures to be improved. A time-based objective might be, "Ninety-five percent of action items will be complete by June 16."

Collectively, these principles define objectives by level, by their connection to each other, by certain conditions on which they rest, and by a desired level of precision.

Programs Without Objectives

Although it's hard to imagine, some projects or programs are implemented without objectives. They might have descriptions—or maybe agendas—but no objectives. The information might be in someone's mind, yet nothing is committed to paper. These situations are certainly undesirable. Objectives give direction, focus, and attention to a project. They clarify the reasons for a project, spell out expectations of those involved, and specify incremental deadlines. Objectives position the program or project for success. These days, objectives also include the amount of money to be made, costs to be reduced, or expense to be avoided. In addition, they must be defined at different levels, be powerful and attention-grabbing, and communicate a strong message.

Problems With Objectives

We have had the opportunity to examine and evaluate hundreds of projects in all types of settings. When conducting an evaluation, including an ROI impact study, we first examine the objectives. In the majority of situations, the owners of the program or project begin the initial meeting by apologizing for the objectives, which are often ill-defined. Below are the most common problems with objectives.

Unclear objectives. An unclear objective might read, "The objective of this project is to develop a diverse, multifaceted, interdisciplinary team that can function in a competitive, challenging, and dynamically changing environment to produce extraordinary and sophisticated outcomes that will dramatically enhance results." What does this mean? Obviously, clarity is needed.

Incomplete objectives. Sometimes objectives are incomplete in that they lack definition. Consider the statement, "The objective of this project is to improve the sales force." Immediately, the question becomes, "So what?" What is lacking about the sales force that would cause it to need improvement?

Is the goal actually to improve sales, market share, profits, customer loyalty, customer satisfaction, or some other measure? Without sufficient detail, the objective is left to interpretation.

Nonspecific objectives. Specificity can be defined at the program level or the individual level. Consider a new compliance program in which the objective is to reduce compliance discrepancies. We need more details. Which discrepancies? By what date? By how much do we want to reduce those discrepancies? At a program level, a more specific objective might be written as, "Reduce compliance discrepancies from $2 million in fines per year to no more than $100,000 by the end of the second year following project implementation." If the compliance discrepancies are at an individual level, then specificity needs to be applied there as well. Conditions for success can add further specificity. For example, the objective might be, "Fines will not increase as business volume increases." The increase in business volume is the condition that makes the objective more specific than if it were written as, "Fines will not increase."

Missing objectives. Certain levels of objectives are frequently omitted, particularly those at higher levels. For example, business impact and ROI objectives are often excluded. If the goal is to add business value, then the objectives should be defined at the business impact level and ROI level when a specific return-on-investment is needed. These objectives are developed along with objectives at the lower levels.

THE POWER OF OBJECTIVES

Objectives are powerful in that they provide direction, focus, and guidance. They create interest, commitment, expectations, and satisfaction. Their effect on different stakeholders varies; they are a necessity, not a luxury. While the power of objectives at the reaction and learning levels is evident, the importance of objectives at higher levels requires additional explanation.

Application/Impact Objectives Drive Programs

Objectives at Level 3 (Application) and Level 4 (Impact) are routinely omitted from projects and programs. Ironically, they are the most powerful levels as they focus on the organization's needs: success with application and the corresponding outcomes. Below we discuss more specifically how these higher levels of objectives fuel a program or project.

Provide focus and meaning to the program. Objectives often present the rationale for a program's existence. They explain the beginning point—the original business need—which translates into a business impact objective. The behavior or performance issues causing the business need translate directly into application objectives. The objectives establish the ultimate expectations, thereby providing direction to stakeholders.

Provide direction to stakeholders. Clear objectives let everyone involved know what must be done to achieve success and what the consequences of that success will be. Actions (applications) and consequences (impact) represent the important outcomes from almost every program. When these objectives are clearly stated, stakeholders can define the actions they need to take to succeed in their role in program implementation.

Define success. Application and impact objectives, clearly expressed with specific criteria and indicators, take the mystery out of the definition of success. By defining success at all levels, the measures taken during evaluation are also defined. Clearly defined measures of success transform into questions asked during the evaluation.

Application/Impact Objectives Enhance Design and Development

A risk not worth taking is sending vague objectives to a program designer or developer. Designers are creative, using their imaginations to build program content. Without clear, specific direction, they will insert their own assumptions regarding the ultimate use of the project (application) and the consequences to the organization (impact). These higher-level objectives have several effects on program development.

Define content issues. The content essentially moves from what participants must learn to make the project successful to what they must do to make it successful. In addition, the application of the content leads to how that success will ultimately be defined. The content shifts from concept and theory to a practical application intended to drive important business outcomes. Although the general principles and facts might remain the same, the situational aspect of the content changes.

Help with design of exercises and activities. When the application and impact objectives are known, the exercises, activities, problems, guides, and checklists in a program can focus on application and impact. The scenarios described in the content form the basis of the exercises. The exercises are focused on application in the work setting. Participants can then envision what they must do to be successful.

Make skill practice and role plays relevant. Skill practices and role plays offer an excellent opportunity to learn and practice new skills. With strong application and impact objectives, the role-play situations are more clearly defined, realistic, and job specific. The mystery of use in the job context has been removed.

Facilitate action plans. One of the most effective ways to measure success is through action planning, in which participants plan what they must do to succeed on the job. When Level 3 and 4 objectives exist, the action planning becomes easier, more specific, and carefully connected to the intended outcomes. Action plans often flow directly from application objectives, removing the temptation to stray from the intended purpose of the project or program.

Make quizzes job related. Quizzes and tests are common measurements of learning success. When the application and impact objectives are clear, there is more context from which to develop job-specific test questions.

Application/Impact Objectives Improve Facilitation

Objectives are the first information reviewed prior to facilitating a meeting or training session, and they define the facilitator's approach in teaching the project or program. They provide guidance for the facilitator to know how to present, what to present, and the context in which to present. More specifically, these higher levels of objectives provide facilitators with the information to do the following.

Show the end result and provide the focus to achieve it. An objective-based approach to facilitation allows the facilitator to show individuals how they will use their learning and the impact it will have.

Focus the discussions on application and impact. The dialogue with the participants is about what they will do and how they will do it on the job, including the challenges and enablers that will either inhibit or help them achieve success. Group discussions, stories, and examples presented by the facilitator help focus on application and impact. The facilitator can describe actual experiences on the job.

Ensure that the facilitator has job-related experience. Because the facilitator must present job-related situations and applications, he or she must fully understand the work. Usually, this means the facilitator must have experience in using what he or she is presenting. This requirement enhances the quality of facilitation and enables specific, job-related discussions about application and impact with the group.

Teach to the test. Facilitators are often accused of teaching to the test. They want to ensure that participants can pass the test. If learning objectives are the sole objectives, the test is based on learning—measuring knowledge and skills acquisition. With application and impact objectives in place, participants are encouraged to understand what they must do, along with the impact and consequences of doing it. This new test scenario drives the application and impact measures. Although the results of the ultimate test will not be known until the post-program follow-up, the facilitator presents the job content so participants can "score well" on the application and impact test that will actually be obtained in the follow-up evaluation.

Application/Impact Objectives Help Participants Understand What Is Expected

Participants need clear direction as to why they are involved in a program or project and what they are expected to do. Essentially, the role of a participant changes with higher levels of objectives. Of course, participants are expected to attend meetings and training, become involved and engaged, and learn. When application and impact objectives are communicated to them, they will realize there is an expectation for them to apply what they learn and that the application of knowledge should reap some benefit. Again, application and impact objectives remove the mystery from the program and the roles within it. Below we specify ways these higher-level objectives help participants understand expectations.

Clarify expectations by detailing what the participant must do. Application objectives define expectations in terms of action—the detail needed when participants use the tools, skills, or knowledge on the job. Application objectives also define tasks that must be completed, meetings that must be held, or forms to be delivered. The action required or expected of the participants is made clear.

Set clear expectations about what the participant must ultimately accomplish. Impact objectives connect the program to the business measures and also to participants' performance. When participants apply what is learned in a project or program, there is a consequence. Often, that consequence is the immediate measure that represents their performance, such as measures of productivity, quality, time, or costs. Participants control or influence these measures.

Define "What's in it for me?" Participants must engage and commit to achieving results and providing data. They need to know what is in it for them, and impact objectives clearly show them. For example, when participants attend a meeting or session on the use of new sales software, the impact objectives clearly indicate the ultimate outcome. These objectives are typically stated in terms of increasing sales, enhancing customer satisfaction, improving market share, increasing customer loyalty, and other important measures. Such objectives clarify what's in it for participants. They want to improve these measures, so such objectives provide incentive to participate.

Explain why the program is being conducted. Individuals may attend a program or participate in a particular project without a clear understanding of why the project exists. Typical questions include, "How would this help the company?" or "How will this help my department?" Application and impact objectives clearly explain the program's purpose and the expected outcome, in addition to what participants must do and ultimately accomplish.

Impact Objectives Excite Sponsors

The sponsors (those who actually fund the program) often request data showing how well the program achieved its goal. Impact measures resonate with executives and program sponsors. It is no secret that executives do not get excited about reaction and learning objectives. They are not as concerned with reactions to a program or even what is learned. Rather, their interest lies in what participants do with what they learn and the ultimate impact on the organization. Impact objectives grab the attention of executives for the following reasons.

Connect the program to the business. Impact objectives connect the program directly to business goals. This linkage piques executive interest and builds program support.

Connect the program to key performance indicators (KPI). Important scorecard measures are goals for the sponsor. Impact objectives often contain executive KPIs, scorecard performance measures, dashboard indicators, or operating results. A deficiency in one or more of these measures often precipitates the need for the program.

Show business value. This is the first opportunity for the sponsor to see value that he or she can appreciate. Business value and attempts to "show the money" make sponsors happy.

Application/Impact Objectives Simplify Evaluation

These high-level objectives pave the way for evaluation by providing the focus and details needed for the evaluator to collect and analyze results. This is perhaps the primary reason, from an accountability perspective, to have higher levels of objectives. Here are some specific things they do to aid evaluation:

> Identify data to be selected in the organization.
> Define specific measures reflected in the data item, distinguishing it from similar or closely related items.
> Suggest the appropriate data collection method to be used. In some cases the measure itself, when clearly defined, suggests how it might be collected.

> ➤ Suggest the source of data by identifying where it is and who has it.
> ➤ Suggest the timing of data collection. The objectives provide hints as to when action is needed and when change will occur, influencing the timing of when data will be collected.
> ➤ Suggest responsibilities to collect data. The definition of data suggests who may be the best person to collect the data. Impact data are sometimes housed in a particular department or function. If data are generated in a field location, someone in the field might be the best person to collect that data.
> ➤ Suggest the appropriate isolation method. Isolating the effects of a program essentially suggests that some technique will always be used to show the cause-and-effect relationship between a program and impact data. When impact data are defined through the development of objectives, the best method to isolate the effects of the program might become evident. The control group arrangement is most credible when it is feasible to use this method. Trend-line analysis is the next most credible method. Other methods are available, including participants' estimates. The measure itself can influence the decision to use one technique versus another.
> ➤ Suggest the appropriate data conversion method. Some measures, when defined clearly, represent measures already converted to money. Other measures need to be converted by experts and specialists. Clearly identifying the measures with impact objectives makes the choice of methods much easier.

In summary, application and impact objectives are extremely valuable for the evaluator. They provide the information necessary to complete the data collection plan and the ROI analysis plan, ultimately making for a more effective, sound evaluation.

All Levels of Objectives Inform the Stakeholders

Collectively, all levels of evaluation help stakeholders understand the program more clearly. All stakeholders need to know not only why the program is being developed, but also about participant reaction, what the participants have learned, what actions they will take, and, ultimately, what they will accomplish.

Such knowledge is particularly critical for managers of participants directly involved in the program. They might not be supportive because they see neither value to which they can relate, nor objectives that reflect their interests. These managers must be able to see how the program connects to key measures. The good news is programs often show value that can make a manager take interest and ultimately support the process. Program objectives provide a preview of what is to come.

CASE STUDIES

Three examples underscore the types and nature of the objectives described in this book. They show how the different levels of objectives are used and how they are stacked to form a chain of impact that should occur as a project or program is implemented. They represent different issues so their application in different areas is clear.

Nations Hotel—Business Coaching

Table 1.2 shows the objectives from a business-coaching program for a global hotel chain (Phillips & Phillips, 2005). In this program, objectives are set at all five levels. The learning and development team was challenged to identify learning needs to help executives find ways to improve efficiency, customer satisfaction, and revenue growth in the company. A key component of the program was the development of a formal, structured coaching program, Coaching for Business Impact. Corporate executives were interested in seeing the actual ROI for the coaching project. An important step in the program design was to develop specific objectives for Levels 1 through 5. These objectives provided the framework to achieve and report success.

Each person receiving coaching selected three out of the five measures listed in the impact objectives, providing flexibility for focus and concentration. These objectives were clearly described to the person being coached in announcements during earlier sessions and throughout the coaching process. The objectives not only provided the framework for collecting data, but they also provided the immediate focus throughout the coaching process.

Global Financial Services—Software Implementation

Global Financial Services Inc. (GFS) is a large international firm that offers a variety of financial services to clients (Phillips, Phillips, Stone, & Burkett, 2007). After analyzing its current sales practices and results, the firm identified the need to manage sales relationships more effectively. A task force comprising representatives from field sales, marketing, financial consulting, information technology, and education and training examined several solutions for improving relationships, including customer-contact software packages.

Table 1.2: Objectives for Coaching for Business Impact

Level 1 Reaction Objectives

After participating in this coaching program, the executives will

> perceive coaching to be relevant to the job

> perceive coaching to be important to job performance at the present time

> perceive coaching to be value added in terms of time and funds invested

> rate the coach as effective

> recommend this program to other executives.

Level 2 Learning Objectives

After completing this coaching program, the executives should improve their understanding of or skills for

> uncovering individual strengths and weaknesses

> translating feedback into action plans

> involving team members in projects and goals

> communicating effectively

> collaborating with colleagues

> improving personal effectiveness

> enhancing leadership skills.

Level 3 Application Objectives

Six months after completing this coaching program, executives should do the following:

> Complete the action plan.

> Adjust the plan accordingly as needed for changes in the environment.

> Show improvements in

  • uncovering individual strengths and weaknesses

  • translating feedback into action plans

  • involving team members in projects and goals

- communicating effectively

- collaborating with colleagues

- improving personal effectiveness

- enhancing leadership skills.

> Identify barriers and enablers to application of knowledge acquired.

Level 4 Impact Objectives

Six months after completing this coaching program, executives should improve at least three specific measures from the following areas:

> sales growth

> productivity/operational efficiency

> direct cost reduction

> retention of key staff members

> customer satisfaction.

Level 5 ROI Objective

The ROI value of the coaching program should be 25%.

The firm chose to implement a software package designed to turn contacts into relationships and relationships into increased sales. The program features a flexible customer database, easy contact entry, a calendar, and a to-do list. The software enables quick, effective customer communication and is designed for use with customized reports. It also has built-in contact and calendar sharing and is Internet ready.

Instead of purchasing software and training for each of the 4,000 relationship managers, GFS evaluated the success of the software on a pilot basis using three groups, each comprising 20 relationship managers. A one-day workshop was designed to teach these relationship managers to use the software. If the program proved successful, yielding the appropriate return-on-investment, GFS planned to implement the program for all its relationship managers. With a focus on results, detailed objectives were developed for the implementation and are shown in Table 1.3.

Table 1.3: Objectives for Software Implementation

Level 1 Reaction Objectives

After reviewing the software, the participants will

> provide a rating of 4 out of 5 on the relevance for specific job applications
> indicate an intention to use the software within two weeks of the workshop (90% target).

Level 2 Learning Objectives

After participating in the workshop, participants will

> score 75 or better on a software test (80% target)
> demonstrate four of these five key features of ACT! with zero errors:
>   • enter a new contact
>   • create a mail-merge document
>   • create a query
>   • send an email
>   • create a call report.

Level 3 Application Objectives

Following the workshop, the participants will

> enter data for 80% of new customer prospects within 10 days of workshop completion
> increase the number of planned follow-up contacts with customers within three months of workshop completion
> use the software daily as reflected by an 80% score on an unscheduled audit of use after one month of workshop completion.

Level 4 Impact Objectives

Three months after implementation, there should be

> reduced number of customer complaints regarding missed deadlines, late responses, and failure to complete transactions
> reduced time to respond to customer inquiries and requests
> increased sales for existing customers
> increased customer satisfaction composite survey index by 20% on the next survey.

Level 5 ROI Objective

Implementation of the new software should achieve a 25% return-on-investment using first-year benefits.

This comprehensive set of objectives provided the appropriate direction and information for the workshop designer, facilitator, participants, senior management team, and task force.

Metro Transit Authority—Absenteeism Control

The Metro Transit Authority (MTA) operates a comprehensive transportation system in a large metropolitan area (Phillips & Phillips, 2002). More than 1,000 buses operate regularly, providing citizens with essential transportation. Many passengers depend on the bus system for their commute to and from work, as well as other travel. MTA employs more than 2,900 drivers to operate the bus system around the clock.

As with many transit systems, MTA experienced excessive driver absenteeism, and the problem continued to grow. Three years prior to implementing a solution, MTA's absenteeism was 7 percent, compared to 8.7 percent in the three-month period prior to implementation—too excessive to keep the transit system operating consistently. Two solutions, along with objectives for both, were developed to correct the problem. The first solution, a low-cost absenteeism policy, allowed a fixed number of absences before termination. The second solution changed the selection process to screen individuals with a history of absenteeism problems. Table 1.4 shows the objectives for these solutions.

Table 1.4: Objectives for Absenteeism Reduction Program

Level 1 Reaction Objectives

After announcing the program, supervisors will

> show support for the No-Fault policy by communicating it to employees including how the policy is applied and the rationale for it

> experience little or no adverse reaction from current employees as the No-Fault absenteeism policy is implemented.

Level 2 Learning Objectives

After implementing this new policy, employees and supervisors should be able to

> describe the No-Fault process

> identify the features and benefits of the No-Fault policy

(continued on next page)

Table 1.4: Objectives for Absenteeism Reduction Program (continued)

> explain the rationale for the No-Fault absenteeism policy and the new screening process.

Level 3 Application Objectives

Immediately after the solutions are implemented, the human resources staff should

> use the new screening process for each selection decision so that a systematic and consistent selection process is in place

> implement and enforce the No-Fault policy consistently throughout all operating units.

Level 4 Impact Objectives

Within the first year this program is completely implemented,

> driver absenteeism should be reduced at least 2%

> the present level of job satisfaction is maintained as the absenteeism initiatives are implemented and applied

> customer service and satisfaction should improve with a reduction in schedule delays caused by absenteeism.

FINAL THOUGHTS

This chapter emphasizes and explains the importance of objectives. While there is general agreement that objectives are necessary, we show how they are critical to program or project success. They help drive the results of projects, clarify expectations, secure commitment, and make for a much more effective program or project. Objectives must be developed with as much specificity as possible, with a clear description of the desired outcomes at higher levels. If business results are desired, a program or project should have application, impact, and, in some cases, ROI objectives. The next chapter will show how objectives are derived.

CHAPTER 2

Where Do Objectives Come From?

O bjectives are based on needs. If needs are not defined clearly and early in the process, a flawed project or program can result, creating inefficiencies and other problems. In this chapter we explore assessment of the various levels of needs, which lead to the levels of objectives. Specifically, we will address payoff needs, business needs, performance needs, learning needs, and preference needs. We'll also examine input needs.

The model presented in Figure 2.1 will prove helpful as analysis begins. In the coming pages, we walk through the process of detailing the needs at six levels, beginning with payoff needs and progressing to input needs. The objectives derived directly from these needs are defined, making a case for multiple levels of objectives that correspond with specific needs. The objectives serve as the transition from needs assessment to evaluation.

PAYOFF NEEDS

The highest level of objectives, return-on-investment, comes from an analysis of payoff needs. This initial step begins with a few crucial questions:

> Is this program worth doing?
> Is the issue worth pursuing?

Figure 2.1: The Objectives Connection

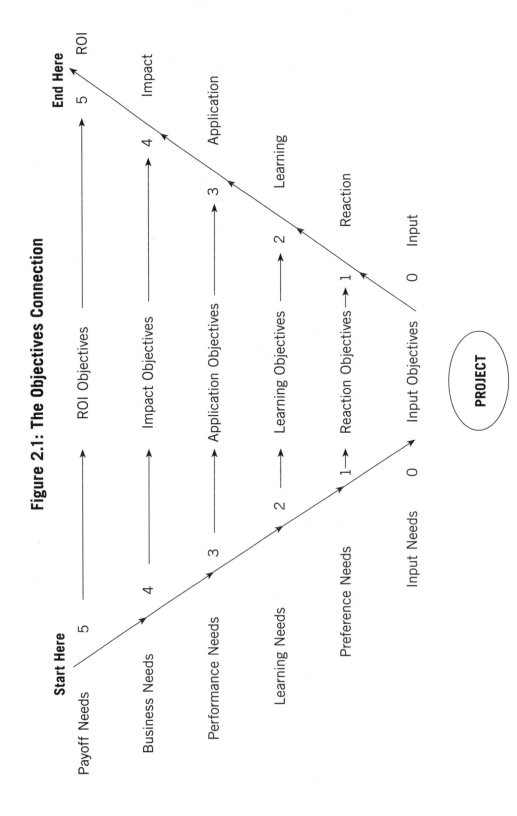

> Is this an opportunity?
> Is it a feasible program?
> What is the likelihood of a positive ROI?

The answers to these questions are obvious for proposed projects or programs that address significant problems or opportunities with potentially high rewards. The questions might take longer to answer for lower-profile programs or those for which the possible payoff is less apparent. In any case, these are legitimate questions, and the analysis can be simple or comprehensive. Figure 2.2 shows the potential payoff in monetary terms. A program's payoff comes in the form of either profit increases or in cost savings (derived from cost reduction or cost avoidance).

Profit increases are generated by programs that improve sales, increase market share, introduce new products, open new markets, enhance customer service, or increase customer loyalty. These should pay off with increases in sales revenue. Other revenue-generating measures include increasing memberships, increasing donations, obtaining grants, and generating tuition from new and returning students—all of which, after taking out the cost of doing business, yield a profit.

However, most programs pay off with cost savings. Savings are generated through cost reduction or cost avoidance. For example, learning and performance that improve quality, reduce cycle time, lower downtime, decrease complaints, prevent employee turnover, and minimize delays are all examples of cost savings. When the goal is solving a problem, monetary value is often based on cost reduction.

Cost-avoidance programs aim to reduce risks, avoid problems, or prevent unwanted events. Some finance and accounting staff view cost avoidance as an inappropriate measure for developing monetary benefits and calculating ROI. However, if the assumptions are correct, an avoided cost (for example,

Figure 2.2: The Payoff Opportunity

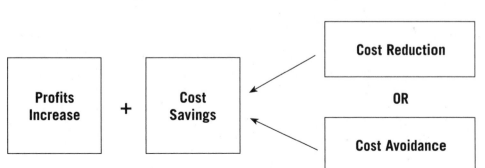

compliance fines) can yield a higher reward than an actual cost reduction. Preventing a problem is more cost-effective than waiting for it to occur and then having to resolve it.

Determining potential payoff is the first step in the needs-analysis process. Closely related is the next step, determining business need, as the potential payoff is often based on improvements or changes in business measures.

Determining the payoff involves two factors: 1) the potential monetary value derived from the business measure's improvement and 2) the approximate cost of the program or project. Ascertaining these monetary values in detail usually yields a more credible forecast of the defined solution. However, this step may be omitted in situations in which the business need must be resolved regardless of the program cost or when resolution of the business need has an obviously high payoff. For example, if the problem involves a safety concern, a regulatory compliance issue, or a competitive matter, then a detailed analysis of the payoff is unnecessary.

Key Questions

A needs analysis should begin with several questions. Table 2.1 presents some questions to ask about a proposed program. The answers to these questions might make the case for proceeding without analysis or indicate the need for additional analysis. The answers could show that the program is not needed. Understanding the implications of moving forward (or not) can reveal the legitimacy of the proposed program.

Table 2.1: Key Questions to Ask About the Proposed Program

➤ Why is this an issue?	➤ Are there multiple solutions?
➤ Who will support the program?	➤ What happens if we do nothing?
➤ Who will not support the program?	➤ How much will the solution(s) cost?
➤ Are there important intangible benefits?	➤ Is a forecast needed?
➤ How can we fund the program?	➤ Is there a potential payoff (positive ROI)?
➤ Is this issue critical?	➤ Is this issue linked to strategy?
➤ Is it possible to correct it?	➤ Is it feasible to improve it?
➤ How much is it costing us?	➤ Can we find a solution?

The good news is, for many potential programs, answers to these questions are readily available. The need might have already been realized and the consequences validated. For example, many organizations with an employee-retention problem within a critical talent group have calculated the cost of employee turnover. This cost is either developed from existing data or secured from similar studies. With this cost in hand, the economic impact of the problem is known. The proposed program's cost can be compared to the problem's cost (in this case, turnover) to get a sense of potential added value. The cost of the program can usually be estimated if a solution has been tentatively identified.

Obvious Versus Not-So-Obvious Payoff

The potential payoff is obvious for some programs, but not so obvious for others. Table 2.2 lists some opportunities with obvious payoffs. Each item is a serious problem that needs attention from executives, administrators, or politicians. For these situations, it would be safe to move ahead to the business needs level rather than invest too much time and resources in analysis of the payoff. After the solution is defined, a forecast may be appropriate.

In other potential programs, however, the issues might be unclear and arise from political motives or biases. Table 2.3 shows opportunities for which

---

Table 2.2: Obvious Payoff Opportunities

> Excessive turnover of critical talent: 35% above benchmark data.

> Very low market share in a market with few players.

> Inadequate customer service: 3.89 on a 10-point customer satisfaction scale.

> Safety record is among the worst in the industry.

> This year's out-of-compliance fines total $1.2 million, up 82% from last year.

> Excessive product returns: 30% higher than previous year.

> Excessive absenteeism in call centers: 12.3%, compared to 5.4% industry average.

> Sexual harassment complaints per 1,000 employees are the highest in the industry.

> Grievances are up 38% from last year.

the payoff isn't as obvious. The not-so-obvious opportunities call for more detail. Some requests are common, as executives and administrators suggest a process change. The requests appear to have the program identified, but without a clear reason as to why. These types of requests could deliver substantial value, but only if they are focused and clearly defined at the start. In our work at the ROI Institute, we have seen many vague requests turn into valuable programs. Sometimes overlooking the vague is a mistake; these requests can result in valuable contributions, as they can lead to critical analysis, ensuring an appropriate focus on development.

The Cost of a Problem

Problems often are expensive. To determine the cost of a problem, its potential consequences must be examined and converted to monetary values. Table

Table 2.3: Not-So-Obvious Payoff Opportunities

> Improve leadership competencies for all managers

> Organize a business development conference

> Establish a project management office

> Provide job training for unemployed workers

> Develop highly effective employees

> Train all team leaders on crucial conversations

> Provide training on sexual harassment awareness for all associates

> Develop an "open-book" company

> Implement the same workout process that GE has used

> Become a technology leader

> Create a great place to work

> Implement a transformation program involving all employees

> Implement a career advancement program

> Create a wellness and fitness center

> Build capability for future growth

> Create an empowered workforce

2.4 shows a list of potential costly problems. Some can easily be converted to money, and some already are. Those that cannot be converted within the resource and time constraints under which you are working are left as intangibles. Inventory shortages are often converted to money based on the direct cost of the inventory, as well as the cost of carrying the inventory. Time can easily be converted into money by calculating the fully loaded cost of the individual's time spent performing unproductive tasks. Calculating time for completing a program, task, or cycle involves measures that can be converted to money. Errors, waste, delays, and bottlenecks can often be converted to money based on the consequences of such problems. Productivity problems, equipment damage, and equipment underuse are other examples of problems that have an apparent cost associated with them.

Examining costs means examining *all* the costs and their implications. For example, the full costs of accidents include not only the cost of lost workdays and medical expenses, but also their effect on insurance premiums, the time required for investigations, damages to equipment, and the time of all employees who address the accident. The cost of a customer complaint includes the cost of the time to resolve the complaint, as well as the value of the item or fee that is adjusted due to the complaint. The most important cost is the loss of future business and goodwill from the complaining customer, plus potential customers who become aware of the issue.

Table 2.4: Potentially Costly Problems

➤ Inventory shortages	➤ Productivity problems
➤ Time savings	➤ Customer dissatisfaction
➤ Excessive employee turnover	➤ Inefficiencies
➤ Errors/mistakes	➤ Excessive conflicts
➤ Employee withdrawal	➤ Excessive direct costs
➤ Waste	➤ Tarnished image
➤ Accidents	➤ Equipment damage
➤ Delays	➤ Lack of coordination
➤ Excessive staffing	➤ Equipment underused
➤ Bottlenecks	➤ Excessive stress
➤ Employee dissatisfaction	➤ Excessive program time

The Value of Opportunity

Just as the cost of a problem can be tabulated in most situations, the value of an opportunity can also be determined. Examples of opportunities include

> ➢ implementing a new process
> ➢ installing new technology
> ➢ upgrading the workforce for a more competitive environment.

In these situations, a problem might not exist, but a tremendous opportunity to get ahead of the competition lies in taking immediate action. Properly placing a value on this opportunity requires considering possible consequences if the project or program is not pursued or taking into account the windfall that might be realized by seizing the opportunity. The monetary value is derived by following the different scenarios to convert specific business impact measures to money. The challenge lies in ensuring a credible analysis. Forecasting the value of an opportunity involves many assumptions, whereas calculating the value of a known outcome is often grounded in a more credible analysis.

BUSINESS NEEDS

Impact objectives are based on business needs. Determining specific business needs is linked to the previous step in the needs analysis, developing the potential payoff. To determine business needs, specific measures must be pinpointed so the business situation is clearly assessed. The term *business* is used in governments, nonprofits, educational institutions, and private sector organizations. Programs and projects in all types of organizations can show business contribution by improving productivity, quality, and efficiency, as well as by saving time and reducing costs.

Business Measures

A business need is represented by a business measure. Any process, item, or perception can be measured, and the measurement is critical to this level of analysis. If the program focuses on solving a problem, program initiators have a clear understanding of that problem and the measures that define the problem. Measures might also be obvious if the program prevents a problem. If the program takes advantage of a potential opportunity, the measures are usually still apparent. If not, a clear, detailed description of the opportunity will help clarify the measure.

The key here is that measures are in the system, ready to be captured for this level of analysis. The challenge is to define and find them economically and swiftly.

Business Measures Represented by Hard Data

Business measures are represented by hard data and soft data. Distinguishing between the two types of data helps in the process of defining specific business measures. Hard data are primary measures of improvement presented in rational, undisputed facts that are usually accumulated. They are the most desired type of data because they're easy to measure and quantify and relatively easy to convert to monetary values. The ultimate criteria for measuring the effectiveness of an organization are hard data such as revenue, productivity, profitability, cost control, and quality assurance.

Hard data are objectively based and represent common, credible measures of performance. They usually fall into four categories, as shown in Table 2.5. These categories—output, quality, cost, and time—are typical performance measures in organizations, including private sector firms, government agencies, nongovernmental organizations, nonprofits, and educational institutions.

Output. Visible hard-data results from a program or project involve improvements in the output of the work unit, section, department, division, or entire organization. All organizations, regardless of type, must have basic measurements of output, such as the number of products sold, patients treated, students graduated, tons produced, or packages shipped. They monitor these factors, so changes can easily be measured by comparing before and after outputs. When programs are expected to drive an output measure, those knowledgeable about the situation can usually make estimates of output changes.

Quality. One of the most significant hard-data categories is quality. If quality is a major concern for an organization, processes are likely in place to measure and monitor it. Thanks in part to the rising popularity of quality improvement processes (such as total quality management, continuous quality improvement, and Six Sigma), pinpointing the correct quality measures—and in many cases placing a monetary value on them—has proven successful. Quality improvement program results can be documented using the standard cost of quality as a value.

Cost. Another important hard-data category is cost improvement. Many projects and programs are designed to lower, control, or eliminate the cost of a specific process or activity. Achieving these cost targets contributes immediately to the bottom line.

Table 2.5: Examples of Hard Data

OUTPUT	QUALITY	COST	TIME
➤ Completion rate	➤ Failure rates	➤ Shelter costs	➤ Cycle time
➤ Units produced	➤ Dropout rates	➤ Treatment costs	➤ Equipment downtime
➤ Tons manufactured	➤ Scrap	➤ Budget variances	➤ Overtime
➤ Items assembled	➤ Waste	➤ Unit costs	➤ On-time shipments
➤ Money collected	➤ Rejects	➤ Cost by account	➤ Time to program completion
➤ Items sold	➤ Error rates	➤ Variable costs	➤ Processing time
➤ New accounts generated	➤ Rework	➤ Fixed costs	➤ Supervisory time
➤ Forms processed	➤ Shortages	➤ Overhead costs	➤ Time to proficiency
➤ Loans approved	➤ Product defects	➤ Operating costs	➤ Learning time
➤ Inventory turnover	➤ Deviation from standard	➤ Program cost savings	➤ Meeting schedules
➤ Patients visited	➤ Product failures	➤ Accident costs	➤ Repair time
➤ Applications processed	➤ Inventory adjustments	➤ Program costs	➤ Efficiency
➤ Students graduated	➤ Time card corrections	➤ Sales expense	➤ Work stoppages
➤ Tasks completed	➤ Incidents	➤ Participant costs	➤ Order response
➤ Output per hour	➤ Compliance discrepancies		➤ Late reporting
➤ Productivity	➤ Agency fees		➤ Lost time days
➤ Work backlog			
➤ Incentive bonus			
➤ Shipments			

Some organizations have an extreme focus on cost reduction. Consider Wal-Mart, whose tagline is "Save Money. Live Better." Wal-Mart focuses on lowering costs on all processes and products and passing the savings to customers. When direct cost savings are used, no efforts are necessary to convert data to monetary value because the costs themselves reflect this value. There can be as many cost items as there are accounts in a cost-accounting system. In addition, costs can be combined in any number of ways to develop the costs needed for a particular program or project.

Time. Time has become a critical measure for today's organizations. Some gauge performance almost exclusively on time. Consider FedEx, whose tagline is "The World on Time." When asked what business FedEx is in, the company's top executives say, "We engineer time." For FedEx, time is so critical that it defines success or failure. Time savings may mean that a program is completed faster than originally planned, a product is introduced earlier, or the time to restore a network is reduced. These savings can translate into lower costs.

Business Measures Represented by Soft Data

Hard data might lag behind changes and conditions in human performance within an organization by many months; therefore, it is useful to supplement hard data with soft data such as attitude, motivation, and satisfaction. Often more difficult to collect and analyze, soft data are used when hard data are unavailable. Soft data are also more difficult to convert to monetary values and are often based on subjective input. They are less credible as a performance measurement and tend to be behavior oriented, but represent important measures just the same. Table 2.6 shows common examples of soft data.

Work habits. Employee work habits are important to the success of work groups. Dysfunctional habits can lead to an unproductive work group, while productive work habits can boost the group's output and morale. Examples of work habits that might be difficult to measure or convert to monetary values appear in Table 2.6. The outcome of some work habits, including employee turnover, absenteeism, and accidents, are in the hard-data category because they're easily converted to monetary values.

Work climate/satisfaction. Several measures reflect employee dissatisfaction. Complaints and grievances sometimes fall in the hard-data category because of their ease of conversion to money. However, most of the items are considered soft-data items. Job satisfaction, organizational commitment, and employee engagement show how attitudes shape the organization. Stress is

Table 2.6: Examples of Soft Data

WORK HABITS
Tardiness
Visits to the dispensary
Violations of safety rules
Communication breakdowns
Excessive breaks

**WORK CLIMATE/
SATISFACTION**
Grievances
Discrimination charges
Employee complaints
Job satisfaction
Organization commitment
Employee engagement
Employee loyalty
Intent to leave
Stress

CUSTOMER SERVICE
Customer complaints
Customer satisfaction

Customer dissatisfaction
Customer impressions
Customer loyalty
Customer retention
Customer value
Lost customers

**EMPLOYEE DEVELOPMENT/
ADVANCEMENT**
Promotions
Capability
Intellectual capital
Programs completed
Requests for transfer
Performance appraisal ratings
Readiness
Networking

CREATIVITY/INNOVATION
Creativity
Innovation
New ideas

Suggestions
New products and services
Trademarks
Copyrights and patents
Process improvements
Partnerships
Alliances

IMAGE
Brand awareness
Reputation
Leadership
Social responsibility
Environmental friendliness
Social consciousness
Diversity
External awards

often a byproduct of a fast-paced work climate. These issues and measurement of these issues are gaining prominence in most organizations.

Customer service. Because increased global competition fosters a greater need to serve and satisfy customers, more organizations are putting into place customer service measures that reflect customer satisfaction, loyalty, and retention. Few measures are as important as those linked to customers.

Employee development/advancement. Employees are routinely developed, assigned new jobs, and promoted. Many soft-data measures can indicate the consequences of crucial activities and processes, such as building capability, creating intellectual capital, enhancing readiness, and fostering networks.

Creativity/innovation. Creativity and innovation are key aspects of successful organizations. A variety of measures can be developed to show the creative spirit of employees and the related outcomes, such as ideas, suggestions, copyrights, patents, and products and services. While the collective creative spirit of employees might be a soft-data item, the outcomes of creativity and innovation qualify as hard data. Still, many executives consider innovation a soft-data item.

Image. Perhaps some of the softest measures relate to image. Executives attempt to increase brand awareness, particularly with sales and marketing programs. Reputation is another measure that is growing in importance. Organizations seek to improve their standings as good employers, good citizens, and good stewards of investors' money. Leadership is probably the most sought-after measure and is influenced by initiatives designed to build leadership within the organization. Image, social responsibility, environmental friendliness, and social consciousness are key outputs of a variety of programs and projects aimed at making the organization well rounded. Diversity is also important for many organizations, which focus programs on increasing diversity of ideas, products, people, and initiatives. Finally, external awards are the outcomes of many activities and programs. Some organizations invest in full-time employees to focus solely on applying for such awards. This particular measure represents the activity, support, and engagement of all employees, including the organization's leadership.

Sources of Impact Data

Sources of impact data, whether hard or soft, are plentiful. They come from routine reporting systems within the organization. In many situations, these items have led to the need for the program or project. Table 2.7 shows a sampling of the vast array of documents, systems, databases, and reports that can be used to select the specific measure or measures to monitor throughout the program.

Table 2.7: Sources of Data	
➤ Department records	➤ Safety and health reports
➤ Work unit reports	➤ Benchmarking data
➤ Human capital databases	➤ Industry/trade association data
➤ Payroll records	➤ R&D status reports
➤ Quality reports	➤ Suggestion system data
➤ Design documents	➤ Customer satisfaction data
➤ Manufacturing reports	➤ Project management data
➤ Test data	➤ Cost data statements
➤ Compliance reports	➤ Financial records
➤ Marketing data	➤ Scorecards
➤ Sales records	➤ Dashboards
➤ Service records	➤ Productivity records
➤ Annual reports	➤ Employee engagement data

Some program planners and team members believe corporate data sources are scarce because the data are not readily available to them, near their workplace, or within easy reach through database systems. With a little determination and searching, however, the data can usually be identified. In our experience, more than 90 percent of the impact measures that matter to a specific program or project have already been developed and are readily available in databases or systems. Rarely do new data collection systems or processes have to be developed.

Collateral Measures

When searching for the proper measures to connect to the program and pinpoint business needs, it's helpful to consider all the possible measures that could be influenced. Sometimes, collateral measures move in harmony with the program. For example, efforts to improve safety might also improve productivity and increase job satisfaction. Thinking about the adverse impact on certain measures also helps. For example, when cycle times are reduced, quality could suffer; or when sales increase, customer satisfaction could deteriorate. Finally, program team members must prepare for unintended consequences and capture them as relevant data items.

PERFORMANCE NEEDS

Application objectives are based on performance needs. In the needs analysis, this step explores reasons the business measure is where it is rather than at the desired level of performance. If the proposed program addresses a problem, this step focuses on the cause of the problem. If the program takes advantage of an opportunity, this step focuses on what is inhibiting the organization from taking advantage of that opportunity.

Analysis Techniques

This step might require a variety of analytical techniques to uncover the causes of the problem or inhibitors to success. Table 2.8 shows a brief listing of these techniques. It is important to relate the issue to the organizational setting, to the behavior of the individuals involved, and to the functioning of various systems. These analytical techniques often use tools from problem-solving, quality assurance, and performance improvement fields. Searching for multiple solutions is also important, because measures are often inhibited for several reasons. Keep in mind the implementation of multiple solutions—whether they should be explored in total or tackled in priority order. The detailed approaches of all the techniques are contained in many references (Langdon, Whiteside, & McKenna, 1999).

Table 2.8: Analysis Techniques

> Statistical process control	> Diagnostic instruments
> Brainstorming	> Focus groups
> Problem analysis	> Probing interviews
> Cause-and-effect diagram	> Job satisfaction surveys
> Force-field analysis	> Engagement surveys
> Mind mapping	> Exit interviews
> Affinity diagrams	> Exit surveys
> Simulations	> Nominal group technique

A Sensible Approach

The resources needed to examine records, research databases, and observe situations and individuals must be taken into account. Analysis takes time, and the use of expert input, both internally and externally, can add to the cost and duration of the evaluation. The needs at this level can vary considerably and might include

> - ineffective behavior
> - dysfunctional work climate
> - inadequate systems
> - disconnected process flow
> - improper procedures
> - unsupportive culture
> - insufficient technology.

These needs have to be uncovered using many of the methods listed in Table 2.8. When needs vary and techniques abound, the risk exists for excessive analysis and cost. Consequently, a sensible approach must be taken. Balance must exist between the level of analysis and availability of resources and time.

LEARNING NEEDS

Learning objectives are based on learning needs. Addressing the job performance needs uncovered in the previous step often requires a knowledge or information component, such as participants and team members learning how to perform a task differently or how to use a new process. In some cases, learning is the principal solution, as in competency development, major technology changes, capability development, and system installations. In these situations, the learning becomes the actual solution.

For other programs, learning is a minor solution and involves simply understanding the process, procedure, or policy. For example, when a new ethics policy is implemented, the learning component requires understanding how the policy works and the participants' role in the policy. In short, a learning solution is not always needed. But all solutions have a learning component.

A variety of approaches measure specific learning needs. Multiple tasks and jobs are usually in a program, and each should be addressed separately.

Subject Matter Experts

One of the most important approaches to determining learning needs is to ask those who understand the process. They can best determine what skills and knowledge are necessary to address the job performance issues defined above. Then it might be possible to understand how much knowledge and how many skills already exist.

Job and Task Analysis

A job and task analysis offers a systematic look at information when a new job is created or when tasks within an existing job description change significantly. Essentially, the analysis collects and evaluates work-related information, determining specific knowledge, skills, tools, and conditions necessary to perform a particular job. The primary objective of the analysis is to gather information about the scope, responsibilities, and tasks related to a particular job or new set of responsibilities. In the context of developing learning needs, this information helps in preparing job profiles and job descriptions. These descriptions, in turn, serve as a platform for linking job requirements to specific information or training needs.

Performing a job and task analysis not only helps individuals who will use the program to develop a clear picture of their responsibilities, but it will also indicate what is expected of them. The amount of time needed to complete a job and task analysis varies from a few days to several months, depending on the complexity of the program. Components include identifying high performers, preparing a job analysis questionnaire, and developing other materials as necessary to collect information. During the job analysis, responsibilities are defined, tasks are detailed, and specific learning requirements are identified (Gupta, 1999).

Observations

Current practices within an organization might have to be observed to understand the context in which the program is implemented. This technique can provide insight into the level of capability, as well as appropriate procedures. Observation is an established and respected data-collection method that can examine workflow and interpersonal interactions, including those between management and team members.

Sometimes, the observer is unknown to those being observed (placed in the environment specifically to observe the current processes). In other instances, the observer previously worked in the environment, but is now in a different role. Another possibility is that the observer is invisible to those being observed. Examples include retail mystery shopping, electronic observation, and temporary employee (observer) placement. It is important to remember that observation can uncover what individuals need to know or do as a program changes.

Demonstrations

In some situations, having employees demonstrate their abilities to perform a certain task or procedure provides valuable insight. The demonstration can be as simple as a skill practice or role play, or as complex as an extensive mechanical or electronic simulation. From this determination of job knowledge, specific learning needs can evolve.

Tests

Testing is not used as frequently as other needs assessment methods, but it can prove highly useful. Employees are tested to find out what they know about a particular situation. Test results help guide learning issues. For example, in one hospital chain, management was concerned that employees were unaware of the company's policy on sexual harassment or what actions constitute sexual harassment. In the early stages of the program analysis, a group of supervisors and managers, the target audience for the program, took a 20-item test about their knowledge of the sexual harassment policy (10 items) and knowledge about sexual harassment actions (10 items). The test scores revealed where insufficient knowledge existed and formed the basis of a program to reduce the number sexual harassment complaints.

Management Assessment

When implementing programs in organizations in which there are existing managers or team leaders, input from the management team might be used to assess the current situation and the knowledge and skills that the new situation requires. This input can be collected through surveys, interviews, or focus groups. It can be a rich source of information about what the users of a new program would need to know to make it a success.

Where the learning component is minor, learning needs are simple. Determining specific learning needs can be time consuming for major programs for which new procedures, technologies, and processes are developed. As in the previous step, it is important not to spend excessive time analyzing at this early stage in the process, but collecting as much data as possible with minimal resources.

PREFERENCE NEEDS

Reaction objectives are based on preferences. This level of needs analysis drives the program features and requirements. Essentially, individuals prefer certain processes, schedules, or activities for the learning and performance improvement program or project. Those preferences define how the particular program will be implemented.

Typical preference needs are statements that define the parameters of the program in terms of timing, content, staffing, location, technology, and extent of disruption allowed. Although everyone involved has certain needs or preferences for the program, implementation is based on the input of several stakeholders rather than that of an individual. For example, participants involved in the program (those who must make it work) might have a particular preference, but their preference could exceed resources, time, and budget requirements. The immediate manager's input may help minimize the amount of disruption and maximize resources. Available funds are also a constraining resource. The urgency for program implementation may create a constraint in the preferences. Those who support or own the program often place preferences around the program in terms of timing, budget, and the use of technology. Because this is a Level 1 need, the program structure and solution will directly relate to the reaction objectives and to the initial reaction to the program.

INPUT NEEDS

Input objectives are based on input needs. This level of analysis is similar to the preference analysis. Here, the basic input requirements are clearly defined. If the program or project is derived from analysis, this analysis would define various parameters and input requirements. If the program or project is addressing compliance, the regulation could define the requirements in terms of timing, content, audience, and even location. Because resources are limited, some constraints might surround budget. Because some projects are urgent, timing issues could come into play. Some projects need to be conveniently located, calling for location requirements. Input needs are often straightforward and come directly from the analysis or the request for the program. Understand clearly that the basis of these requirements captures all the needs, and they quickly and straightforwardly translate into input objectives.

FINAL THOUGHTS

Objectives are based on clearly defined needs, derived from careful analysis of the problem, opportunity, or requirement that led to the project or program. By considering the needs stacked on different levels, ranging from payoff needs to input needs, the complete profile is developed, which leads to a profile of objectives. Not every project or program should be subjected to all of these analyses. Some we base solely on learning needs. Others might be based strictly on preference needs, which is the case for many programs in the meetings and events arena, for example. The important issue is to take a rational, logical approach when determining needs and, ultimately, objectives. The remainder of the book focuses on how to construct the objectives that evolve from these needs. We will begin with input objectives, Level 0.

CHAPTER 3

Input Objectives

Inputs are activities that make up the project or program. They are often dictated by a variety of stakeholders. Inputs include the required resources, cost, and scope for a project or program. Often developed at project conception, they're not always communicated clearly to all stakeholders, particularly those directly involved. This chapter describes the importance of developing input objectives and provides several examples.

ARE INPUT OBJECTIVES NECESSARY?

Think about a particular project or program. At conception, certain parameters are described or envisioned. Maybe the project is intended for only one division or group of employees and must be completed by a specific deadline or within a firm budget. These parameters help define the scope and nature of the project. Essentially, the parameters describe the inputs in detail, outlining what the organization plans to do, with and for whom to do it, and how much it will cost. Are they necessary? Yes. Are they listed as precise objectives for everyone to see? Not necessarily. Certainly some document or agreement would contain these objectives. The overriding question is this: Does the stakeholder need this information? For some, it might be helpful to ensure that all stakeholders have it, particularly those directly involved. When in doubt, we prefer to err on the side of full disclosure. The more information shared, the less likely misunderstandings will occur.

HOW TO CONSTRUCT INPUT OBJECTIVES

Input objectives follow the same basic design criteria as described in chapter 1. They should be simple, straightforward, precise, and indicate timing and focus. It is helpful at the beginning of a project to write objectives that define the inputs in terms of issues such as resources, people involved, timing, location, and other constraints on the process and delivery. Here are a few possibilities.

TOPICS FOR INPUT OBJECTIVES

Volume/Staffing

The most obvious place to start with input objectives is the people involved. An objective may focus on the number of participants planned in a formal program and may be divided into demographic categories. For example, an objective may read, "Forty percent of participants will be females with five years of experience." Some organizations want to ensure that upward mobility exists for all employees, particularly female. The glass ceiling still exists in many organizations, and ensuring that women can take advantage of opportunities requires not only learning and development programs, but also an appropriate number of female participants.

Extending beyond gender and counting participants by other diverse characteristics is another consideration. Programs must be in place to ensure that all employees are involved and have equal opportunity to pursue their careers. Still other parameters might be considered, such as length of service. Individuals with the least amount of tenure should receive the most development. Unfortunately, this is not the case in some organizations.

Project staffing might constitute an objective. Total number of individuals involved in a project is sometimes an issue. An input objective might reflect a maximum or minimum number of people, as well as their job status, such as part-time versus full-time employees. For example, in a technology project, the staffing level input objective was that no more than 15 full-time staffers would take part in the project at any given time. Project teams can also be counted. These teams can be assigned by division, department, function, or even different region.

Scope

Scope establishes the limits of a project. These objectives might place boundaries on implementation, participants, or departments directly involved, as well as the specific function or content explored. A project's scope might also define the total number of hours to be included or the nature of the work to be done. Defining the scope prevents "scope creep," in which a project starts out with a narrow focus of one or two topics or areas, and then mushrooms, requiring excessive time, effort, and even money.

Audience/Coverage

Perhaps the most important objective category is the coverage by jobs, job groups, and even functional areas. For example, with the current focus on talent management, some organizations implement projects to address critical talent coverage. They do this by defining critical talent and setting objectives for the number of project participants in the critical talent categories.

Another way to address audience is by a particular function, from research and development through sales, marketing, and customer support. This objective identifies the parts of the organization involved in programs. Coverage might also be defined by specific job levels, such as executives, managers, professionals, and nonexempt employees. Many organizations are concerned about particular job groups, such as first-level supervisors. For example, as an individual job category, this important group in an organization should have many learning and development opportunities. When they use their skills on the job, the effect is multiplicative. As they work with their teams, they drive team performance.

Coverage can also focus on specific strategic initiatives. Projects and programs often are aligned with particular strategic objectives, supporting them with implementation issues. An objective might include the total hours and people included in a particular strategic area. This shows current alignment with an important strategy and can be revealing. When particular strategic areas have little or no coverage with programs, action should be taken to devote more resources directly to those areas.

A final way to represent coverage with input objectives is to focus on particular operational problems. An input objective might be written as, "All customer service staff will be involved in addressing our customer service problem." Several projects or programs aimed at customer service improvement could help meet this objective.

Timing

Timing objectives indicate when certain tasks will be accomplished, milestones will be reached, or an entire project will be completed. These objectives might dictate when certain individuals become involved in the project or even the timing in which the project team is paid. Timing is critical. Without it, accountability might be absent and misunderstandings might prevail.

Duration

The length of time participants are involved in a project is a common input objective. Some organizations track the total hours of involvement to create an impressive image. A more appropriate measure might be the hours spent per person, targeting a specific amount of time for a particular job or job group. Other organizations track the number of hours involved by various diversity groups, including age, gender, and race. For example, for learning and development, some organizations make a commitment to an average number of hours per person. While this is an admirable goal, it might create more activity than actual change.

Setting objectives for the duration of participation is important for learning and development, human resources, coaching, consulting, and meetings and events. These objectives usually focus on the total duration of the program; for example, organizing a three-day conference, conducting a six-month coaching program, or providing a three-day, new-employee indoctrination.

Budget/Costs

The most logical input objective is cost. The cost of projects and programs is increasing, creating more pressure to know how and why money is spent. The total cost of a project is required, which means calculating indirect as well as direct costs. Fully loaded cost information is used to manage resources, develop standards, measure efficiencies, and examine alternative delivery methods.

Project cost sources must be considered. The three major categories of these sources are found in Table 3.1. Project staff expenses usually represent the greatest percentage of costs and are sometimes transferred directly to the client or project sponsor. The second major cost category is participant expenses, both direct and indirect. These costs are not identified in many programs, yet they reflect a significant amount of the total expenditures. The third cost source is payments to external organizations. These include payments directly to hotels and conference centers, equipment suppliers, and services used for the program. As the table shows, some of these cost categories are often understated. Accounting records should track and reflect the costs from these three different sources.

Table 3.1: Sources of Costs	
Source of Costs	**Cost-Reporting Issues**
1. Project staff expenses	A. Costs are usually accurate.
	B. Variable expenses may be underestimated.
2. Participant expenses (direct and indirect)	A. Direct expenses are usually not fully loaded.
	B. Indirect expenses are rarely included in the costs.
3. External expenses (equipment and services)	A. Sometimes understated.
	B. May lack accountability.

Another key method of developing cost objectives follows the natural project progression. Figure 3.1 shows the typical project cycle, beginning with the initial analysis and assessment and progressing to the evaluation and reporting of results. Input objectives for costs can be developed for each of these steps.

The specific items to be included in the program costs must be defined. Input from the finance and accounting staff, the project team, and management might be needed. The recommended cost categories for a fully loaded, conservative approach to estimating costs are

> needs analysis and assessment
> design and development costs
> acquisition costs (in lieu of development costs, many organizations purchase programs)
> delivery/implementation costs (five categories)
  • salaries of facilitators and coordinators
  • program materials and fees
  • travel, lodging, and meals
  • facilities (external and in-house)
  • participants' salaries and benefits
> evaluation costs
> overhead costs.

Figure 3.1: Project Functions and Cost Categories

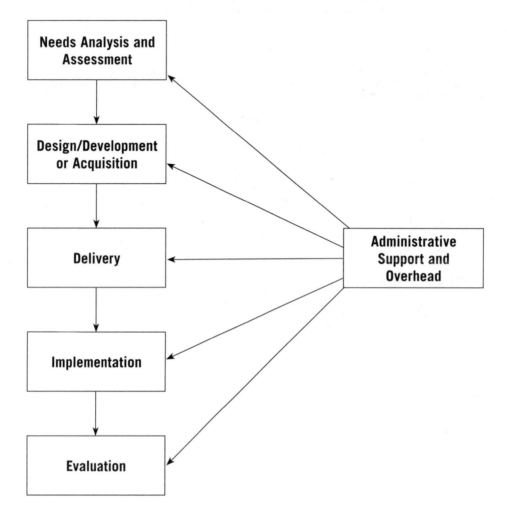

Efficiencies

Efficiency is measured in different ways and from different viewpoints. One of the first measures is efficient use of the project team. An objective can come in the form of the number of participants per project team member. From an efficiency standpoint, this number should be as high as possible. Efficiency is also reported as content provided per project team member or the average cost per content hour provided. Other efficiency measures focus on the time to accomplish certain tasks—the average time to conduct a needs assessment or to design an hour of content. Other time objectives include the time an individual takes to complete a program or the total cycle time from a request to launch a program to delivery of that program.

Content

Input objectives focus on content in various ways. For example, in learning and development, the percentage of content devoted to a particular area is significant. In the American Society for Training & Development's benchmarking forum (the more than 200 organizations considered best-practice organizations), data show that more than 50 percent of the content is industry specific, IT systems oriented, and business practices oriented. This underscores the shift in learning content as more organizations focus on technology and job- and industry-specific activities.

For some meetings and events and conferences, content naturally serves as an input objective. For compliance in an ethics program, portions of the content must focus on the regulations themselves. In executive coaching, an objective might require a certain percentage of content focus on business impact.

Project Origin

An often overlooked input objective focuses on why programs are requested in the first place. Too many programs are implemented for the wrong reasons—or at least questionable reasons. Understanding where and how a project originated can provide insight into the reason it was implemented. Table 3.2 shows the tracking of reasons for programs at a large financial services firm. What is revealing in this example is that more than 50 percent of the programs are implemented for questionable reasons (see reasons 1, 2, 4, 10, and 11). By tracking this information over time, executives can see how the origin of projects is changing or should change in the future. Objectives might be based on the desired analysis or reason for the project. For example, in a hospital chain, a request for a sexual harassment prevention program to lower the number of claims had an objective to "proceed with a solution after the cause of excessive claims has been identified."

Delivery

One of the most interesting and mysterious processes is the way in which a project or program is delivered to an organization. Although strides are being made to transform traditional delivery processes into those that are more technology based, progress has been slower than most experts forecasted. An organization attempting to make dramatic shifts in delivery needs to keep an eye on technological advancement. For learning and development, delivery is shifting from traditional in-person, facilitator-led delivery to e-learning and, more specifically, blended learning.

Table 3.2: Sources of New Projects and Programs	
1. Management requests it.	23%
2. The topic is a trend.	13%
3. An analysis was conducted to determine need.	12%
4. Other organizations in industry have implemented it.	11%
5. It supports new equipment, procedures, or technology.	10%
6. A regulation requires it.	8%
7. It supports new policies and practices	6%
8. It supports other processes, such as Six Sigma, transformation, continuous process improvement, etc.	6%
9. It appears to be a serious problem.	5%
10. A best-selling book has been written about it.	4%
11. Staff members think it is needed.	2%

Delivery includes not just the use of technology, but also the efficiency with which the project will be implemented throughout the organization. This is particularly important when a project is implemented on a pilot basis and the results are disseminated throughout the organization. When it comes to creating a new system, procedure, or policy, much of the success hinges on how and when it is implemented throughout the organization. Capturing expectations with objectives is critical to success.

Location

Projects and programs sometimes require particular locations. For example, in the meetings and events industry, an event might call for a particular type of site, or the preference might be the East Coast, West Coast, or a resort. Location can be dictated by whether the project is internal or external. If there is a required location, it is stated as an objective.

Disruption

Disruption of normal work activities almost always presents a concern for project leaders. They often design programs to minimize disruption, which might include setting an objective to ensure that individuals' regular duties are not affected by participation in the program. For example, a requirement in implementation of a Six Sigma program (a quality improvement process) was that completion of the projects to reach green belt and black belt status should not disrupt normal work activities on the job.

Technology

In most cases, technology is used to coordinate, design, deliver, or manage a project. Sometimes technology should be defined as an input parameter. For example, an objective might require that parts of the project or program be conducted virtually using Microsoft Office Live Meeting. Another objective might require that all participants network with each other through tools such as LinkedIn or IBM's Lotus Connection. Technology makes a critical contribution to the success of projects and programs. It should be defined upfront with other appropriate objectives.

Outsourcing/Contracting

An increasing number of organizations outsource some or all projects and programs. As an organization moves in this direction, outsourcing objectives might be needed. For example, an objective in the program development stage might require that external contractors develop no more than 50 percent of the program. Internal staff develops the remainder. Another objective might reflect outsourcing of delivery, detailing the percentage of the program delivered by external services compared to internal sources.

HOW TO USE INPUT OBJECTIVES

Input objectives are very basic and clearly define the project from the outset. There are four key issues related to input objectives.

Project Conception

Projects are conceived with input objectives in mind. Whether an initiative grew out of an analysis, a deteriorating problem, or simply an executive request, the process usually includes input objectives. For example, when an executive asks that a project be implemented, that request usually includes input objectives around timing, cost, and scope. When a regulation creates a need for a project, many of the input objectives are defined by the regulation.

When a detailed analysis is completed, the results often reveal the input objectives. The challenge is to ensure that all relevant input items are addressed during the conception stage so that all key stakeholders understand what's involved.

Project Budgeting

Many input objectives define cost items. One input objective is the actual cost itself. Other input objectives have a tremendous effect on the cost; for example, the technology to be used, the location of the project, and the number of people involved are huge cost items. Even determining the amount of disruption of work allowed has an impact on the cost. Consequently, detail of the input objectives provides a proper backdrop to calculate the overall budget for the project.

Project Planning

As the project is designed, developed, delivered, implemented, and analyzed, the inputs provide the starting point for project planning. They often define who is involved, when they're involved, and to what extent they're involved. They also indicate other factors or processes involved in the project. Planning is critical, and input objectives are the beginning of the planning process.

Project Support

Input objectives also provide information to support the project properly. They alert individuals as to what's needed and when it's needed. To a certain extent, they also define some of the critical success factors, such as achieving deadlines and budget performance. Many others must support the project, but might not be directly involved. For example, participants' managers are in a position to influence outcomes significantly. Their support is critical, and the input objectives clearly define who is involved and why they're involved.

EXAMPLES

Table 3.3 presents a sample of input objectives spread over the topics addressed in this chapter.

Table 3.3: Examples of Input Objectives

This program must be:	Parameter
› Conducted with at least 100 participants per month	Volume/Staffing
› Completed with an internal team of no more than 12 full-time equivalents	Volume/Staffing
› Implemented as a pilot project only	Scope
› Conducted in the product testing phase only	Scope
› For sales staff only	Audience/Coverage
› For new exempt employees	Audience/Coverage
› Initiated by March 1	Timing
› Completed by September 1	Timing
› Conducted in less than three days	Duration
› Completed with no more than three hours in a meeting	Duration
› Within 3% of each region's budgeted amount	Budget/Costs
› Less than $1,000 in direct cost per person	Budget/Costs
› Designed at a ratio of no more than 10 hours per one hour of content	Efficiency
› Devoted to advanced negotiation skills	Content
› Focused on new technology 80% of the time	Content
› Originated based on thorough needs analysis	Origin
› Implemented to support new processes and practices	Origin
› Implemented with blended learning	Delivery
› Conducted at a resort on the Gulf Coast	Location
› Implemented in the Midwest only	Location
› Implemented without disruption of work	Disruption
› Seamless with customers	Disruption
› Integrated with existing online systems	Technology
› Implemented using a virtual project management tool	Technology
› Implemented with no more than 50% outsourcing	Outsourcing

FINAL THOUGHTS

This chapter defines input objectives, the first category of objectives. Though always necessary, they're often underappreciated and undercommunicated. The more detailed their definition, the better. Input objectives touch on several key elements, including timing, budgeting, scope, duration, coverage, and delivery. From some perspectives, these objectives are obvious and are necessarily defined at the creation of the project; however, too often they stop short of the detail needed. When it comes to objectives, too much detail is rarely a problem.

From the input level, we move to other categories of objectives that define the success of projects or programs. The next chapter focuses on another important set of objectives—reaction objectives.

EXERCISE: WHAT'S WRONG WITH THESE INPUT OBJECTIVES?

This brief exercise will bring the concepts of input objectives into focus. Table 3.4 presents objectives that need improvement. Take a few minutes to examine each objective. What concerns you about each one and how it is stated? Responses to this exercise are provided in Appendix A.

Table 3.4: What's Wrong With These Input Objectives?

1. The project should be completed on schedule.

2. The project should be inexpensive and use the latest technology.

3. The project should be well received by all stakeholders involved.

4. The project will involve all employees with frontline responsibility.

5. The project should minimize the disruption of regular work.

CHAPTER 4

Reaction Objectives

Any project leader, program coordinator, or facilitator desires a positive reaction to his or her efforts. Unfortunately, the terms *positive* and *reaction* are vague. Sometimes a specific reaction to the project or program is desired. While Level 0 (Input) objectives set the scope of the program, Level 1 (Reaction) objectives tell us what initial success to expect. Projects can go astray with an adverse reaction. If participants view program content or project intent as irrelevant, the likelihood that anything will change is slim. Consequently, defining the desired reaction through a reaction objective is an important step toward ensuring results that meet stakeholder expectations. This chapter explores topics for reaction objectives, as well as how they are constructed and used.

ARE REACTION OBJECTIVES NECESSARY?

Some might argue that reaction objectives are always understood and do not need to be spelled out. Of course we want a favorable reaction. However, reaction objectives should be stated for three fundamental reasons.

First, reaction is a vague, subjective construct that needs clarification if we want to ensure we get the reaction we seek. Objectives provide the basis for this clarification. For example, at times the reaction objective is based on motivating participants. In other situations, the reaction objective explains why they're there. So the reaction objective answers the question, "What's in it for me?" Sometimes the objective is to avoid a negative reaction, because the project or program is controversial. At other times, reaction objectives show that the program is necessary and appropriate for members of the target audience and their role in the organization. Definition is needed.

Second, programs can fail if the reaction is unfavorable (that is, the desired reaction is not achieved). An example is a project perceived to be controversial because it changes the way in which the group works by adding extra tasks to the schedule or removing freedoms that the group previously enjoyed. These situations can provoke a negative reaction; therefore, the objective would be to present the project in a logical, rational way so participants can see that it is necessary. At best, this approach would foster an understanding of the importance of the new approach with participants' willingness to apply necessary actions. At worst, it would prevent participants from sabotaging the success of the project. If the project were perceived to be negative, its value in terms of learning application and impact would be practically dead because of the adverse reaction. Consider a traditional learning and development program. If participants don't find it useful or helpful, the experience will be generally unpleasant, possibly causing them to miss important concepts necessary for application and, ultimately, impact. Hence, there would be little to no learning, which then leads to little or no application or business impact.

Third, clearly defined reaction objectives are needed because they represent the first level of project or program success. The chain of impact begins at this level. While reaction is undervalued by sponsors and clients, the objectives are important to those people intimately involved in implementing the program. The irony is that in most projects, reaction is captured, but objectives have not been developed. This leaves the data derived from an evaluation, to some extent, useless. The basis for evaluation is derived from the objectives. Without them, how can success be determined?

The question remains: Are reaction objectives absolutely necessary? It depends. Do you want to measure reaction and hope the results are understood? Or do you want meaningful measures that will provide some direction toward higher levels of success? If you answer "yes" to the latter, then you need reaction objectives.

HOW TO CONSTRUCT REACTION OBJECTIVES

Developing reaction objectives is quite straightforward. They're easy to develop and easy to measure, taking very little time. There are five issues to keep in mind when developing reaction objectives.

Descriptions of Perception

By definition, a reaction objective is based on the perception of those involved in the program or project. Perception is essentially a measure of how someone reacts to the objective. Descriptions of perception vary. The key is to be clear on what perception is needed to ensure participants are engaged and willing to acquire the knowledge, skills, or information required to change what needs to change. Table 4.1 shows the different keywords for objectives to reflect reaction.

Table 4.1: Keywords for Reaction Objectives		
➤ Perceive	➤ Impression	➤ Leaning
➤ React	➤ Deem	➤ Stance
➤ Rate	➤ Grade	➤ Opinion
➤ Attitude	➤ Feel	➤ Regard
➤ Envision	➤ Inclination	➤ Think
➤ Interpret	➤ Deduce	➤ Consider
➤ View		
Example: Participants should *perceive* this program to be relevant to their work, as indicated by an average of 4 out of 5 on a 5-point scale.		

Specificity

Sometimes objectives reflect a certain degree of reaction. If a 2-point scale is used (yes or no, favorable or unfavorable), planning for a percentage of "yes" or "favorable" responses may be the precision that's needed. On a 5-point scale, measuring the percentage rating 4 out of 5 would be appropriate. Sometimes even decimal points are used (that is, 4.2 out of 5), although the incremental parts of a 5-point scale might have no actual meaning from a quantitative standpoint. Sometimes a 7- or 10-point system is used in setting objectives and measuring success, although a 10-point scale is usually not the most appropriate for this type of evaluation. Five to 7 points represents enough variance in the scale to give respondents the choices they need. The idea, however, is to identify a specific degree of success, regardless of the type of question or scale.

This specificity may be based on historical results and then correlated with a specific level of performance. Specificity of the measure may also represent a slight increase over the typical reaction results. Sometimes the degree of success is arbitrary due to insufficient baseline information. In either case, it is important to set the specific desired measure of success and know why you have set it at that level.

Number of Objectives

While the principal issue in developing objectives is precision, the challenge is to avoid having too many reaction objectives. After all, in the success value chain, reaction is perhaps the weakest level of feedback, at least from an executive viewpoint. Overkill needs to be avoided. Identify only the most critical reaction issues, and develop specific targets of success to make the measure meaningful.

Content Focus Versus Noncontent Focus

An important consideration in developing reaction objectives is to obtain data about the content of the program. Too often, feedback data reflect aesthetic issues that may not reflect the substance of the program at hand. Take, for example, an attempt to show the value of a sales and marketing program that focused on client development. The audience consisted of relationship managers—those individuals who have direct contact with the customer. This particular program was designed to discuss product development and a variety of marketing and business development strategies. An appropriate set of reaction objectives would include those that represent content or the presentation of content on product development, marketing, and business strategies. Table 4.2 shows the comparison of measures explored on a reaction questionnaire. The traditional way to evaluate these activities is to focus on noncontent issues. As the table shows, the column on the left represents areas important to activity surrounding the session, but few measures related to content. The column on the right shows more focus on content, with only minor input on issues such as the facilities and service provided. This is not to imply that the quality of the service, the atmosphere of the event, and the quality of the speakers are unimportant. They are and should be addressed appropriately. A more important set of data, however, is detailed information about the perceived value of the program, the importance of the content, and the planned use of material or a forecast of the impact—indicators that positive results did and will occur. This is underscored by the shift occurring in the meetings and events industry, which is moving from measuring entertainment to measuring meaningful reaction, learning, and even application, impact, and ROI.

Table 4.2: Comparison of Content Versus Noncontent Objectives	
Focus on Noncontent Issues	**Focus on Content Issues**
➤ Demographics	➤ Facilities
➤ Location	➤ Service
➤ Transportation	➤ Relevance of materials
➤ Registration	➤ Importance of content to job success
➤ Logistics	➤ Timing of program
➤ Hotel service	➤ Appropriate use of time
➤ Media	➤ Amount of new information
➤ Food	➤ Quality of facilitators
➤ Breaks and refreshments	➤ Perceived value of program
➤ Cocktail reception	➤ Contacts made
➤ Facilitator	➤ Planned use of material
➤ Materials/topics	➤ Forecast of impact
➤ Overall satisfaction	➤ Overall satisfaction

Key Concepts

Table 4.3 shows the criteria involved in creating reaction objectives. The table also presents 10 of the most important reaction questions to ask. Along with these questions, additional topics are addressed in reaction objectives, as described in the next section.

TOPICS FOR REACTION OBJECTIVES

Many topics serve as targets for reaction objectives, because so many issues and processes are involved in a typical project or program. Reaction is important for almost every major issue, step, or process to make sure outcomes are successful. Table 4.4 shows typical topics of objectives. The list reveals possible reactions to

Table 4.3: Developing Reaction Objectives

CRITERIA FOR THE BEST REACTION OBJECTIVES

> Identify important and measurable issues

> Are attitude based, clearly worded, and specific

> Underscore the linkage between attitude and the success of the program

> Represent a satisfaction index from key stakeholders

> Can predict program success

KEY QUESTIONS

> How relevant is the program?

> How important is the program?

> Are the facilitators effective?

> How appropriate is the program?

> Is this new information?

> Is the program rewarding?

> Will you implement the program?

> Will you use the concepts/advice?

> What would keep you from implementing objectives from the program?

> Would you recommend the program to others?

a project or program, beginning with readiness and moving through a variety of content-related issues to recommendations to others.

Ready

Many programs fail because of inadequate preparation by participants or perhaps involvement of the wrong participants. An objective could focus on ensuring that the right people are involved and that they are prepared for the project.

Useful

Although this might seem apparent, the project or program must be useful to participants. In far too many situations, it is not useful, and its benefit to the organization isn't clear. Consequently, usefulness is an important reaction objective.

Necessary

For some projects, it's important for participants to realize the need for an initiative. This type of objective might be appropriate for implementation of a new ethics program or cost-containment project for health care, as employees must see that action is necessary.

Appropriate

A project or program needs to be appropriate for the situation. Sometimes mismatches occur between the program and the problem. Participants need to see that this is the appropriate action to take given the situation at hand.

Motivational

Some projects or programs are designed to motivate employees to improve performance or reach a goal. The important issue is to make sure participants are motivated to take action. This is particularly helpful for reward systems, meetings and events, and leadership development programs or projects.

Rewarding

Some projects need to be rewarding for participants and other key stakeholders. This is particularly true for projects such as an employee suggestion system

Table 4.4: Topics for Reaction Objectives

➤ Ready	➤ Powerful	➤ Intent to use
➤ Useful	➤ Leading edge	➤ Planned action
➤ Necessary	➤ Just enough	➤ New information
➤ Appropriate	➤ Just for me	➤ Overall evaluation
➤ Motivational	➤ Efficient	➤ Content
➤ Rewarding	➤ Easy/difficult	➤ Delivery
➤ Practical	➤ Service-related	➤ Facilities/environment
➤ Valuable	➤ Relevance	➤ Facilitator/team leader evaluation
➤ Timely	➤ Importance	➤ Recommend to others

where cash rewards are provided for submitting a suggestion; a pay-for-skills program where employees are rewarded with promotion if they learn new skills; or a compensation system that rewards employees directly for performance. Employees must see these projects as rewarding; otherwise, their involvement may be limited.

Practical

In a world of complex workplace issues, practicality is imperative. Projects or programs should provide a practical application, devoid of unnecessary theoretical issues.

Valuable

One of the most powerful objectives focuses on the value of a project. Participants need to see value, as it benefits both them and the organization. Value can be expressed in terms of a good investment by the employer or a good investment of the participants' time. In some situations, program owners want participants to view the program as valuable enough that they will take the appropriate actions during and after the program.

Timely

Some projects need to be perceived as timely—not too early and not too late. This is particularly important for new technology, new tools, or training for new jobs. Employees see these projects as timely in their implementation. When employees are promoted into new jobs, they want new skills and new technologies. The programs and projects that offer these skills and technologies should be timely so employees can apply them in their new role.

Powerful

To achieve dramatic improvement or urgent action, a project might need to be perceived as powerful. This is particularly important for breakthrough processes, exciting technology, and new approaches to old problems (that is, new content and completely new skills). Participants need to see this material as making a powerful impact on them and their work life.

Leading Edge

Some projects are implemented to stay ahead of others—to stay on the leading edge of technology or processes when compared to competitors. This is important when new systems are implemented and new products are developed. Employees and others involved need to see them as advanced or visionary.

Just Enough

Some projects contain more information than participants want to use or be involved with—too many unneeded or unwanted parts. An ideal project or program has just enough information. This is a key objective for training programs where information is provided at a rate that allows employees to learn what they need to do and nothing more.

Just for Me

Some projects need to be tailored to individual participants. This is helpful for programs that are specific to an individual's needs, as in training, coaching, or performance improvement processes.

Efficient

All programs need to be implemented efficiently. Those involved need to see organization and precise execution. People do not react favorably to inefficiency. They must see the efforts to make a project smooth and efficient.

Easy/Difficult

Project participants need to find the effort easy or at least not too difficult to accomplish. If it becomes too difficult, participants avoid it, or do it improperly, resulting in problems. In some cases, there needs to be an appropriate balance between too easy and too difficult.

Service-Related

A lot of projects involve support groups or others who provide service to the team. Service could mean making the process more conducive to work, the atmosphere more conducive to learning, or the setting more enjoyable and entertaining. This is particularly true for meetings and events, where the service provided for the hotel is a critical issue. It's also important when project leaders and other staff provide excellent feedback and service to support all participants.

Relevance

Participants want to learn information, skills, and knowledge that is relevant to their work. Consequently, it is helpful to explore the relevance of the program or project to the participants' current work or future responsibilities. If it is relevant, more than likely it will be used.

Importance

Participants need to see that the content is important to their job success. This provides an answer to "What's in it for me?"

Intent to Use

Asking participants about their intentions to use the content or material can be helpful. The extent of planned use can be captured, along with the expected frequency of use and the anticipated level of effectiveness when using the information, skills, and knowledge. Intent to use usually correlates to actual use and is important for enhancing the transfer of learning to the job.

Planned Action

While asking participants the extent to which they intend to use knowledge, skills, and information acquired during a program or project is important and is often a predictor of actual use, it is sometimes important to capture their actual planned actions. An objective reflecting the need for participants to identify three to five planned actions gives them focus throughout the program.

New Information

In too many situations, programs simply rehash old material or address the same problem. Sorting out what is considered new information and what is old information can be helpful.

Overall Evaluation

Almost all organizations capture an overall satisfaction rating, which reflects participants' overall satisfaction with the project or program. While this might have very little value in terms of understanding the real issues and the program's relationship to future success, comparing one program to another and with the programs over time might be helpful. Because the data can be easily misinterpreted and misused, other areas might provide a better understanding of needed adjustments or improvements.

Content

Program content includes the principles, steps, facts, ideas, and situations presented in the program. The content is critical, and participant input is necessary.

Delivery

Because programs can be delivered in a variety of ways, objectives about the appropriateness and effectiveness of the delivery method might prove helpful. Whether delivery is by case studies, coaching, discussion, lectures, exercises, or role plays, understanding the effectiveness of the process from the perspective of the consumer is important.

Facilities/Environment

Sometimes, the environment is not conducive to learning. Feedback can identify issues that need attention. These types of data include the learning space, the comfort level in the learning environment, and other environmental issues, such as temperature, lighting, and noise. A word of caution: If nothing can be done about the learning environment, then data surrounding the environment should not be collected.

Facilitator/Team Leader Evaluation

Perhaps one of the most common uses of reaction data is to evaluate the facilitator. If properly implemented, helpful feedback data that participants provide can be used to make adjustments to increase effectiveness. The issues usually involve preparation, presentation, level of involvement, and pacing of the process. Some cautions need to be taken, however, because facilitator evaluations can be biased either positively or negatively. Other evidence might be necessary to provide an overall assessment of facilitator performance.

Recommend to Others

When participants are voluntarily involved in projects and programs, it is important to create a need for still others to participate. If this is the case, having an objective that focuses on the extent to which employees recommend the project or program to others can be extremely helpful. Word-of-mouth recommendations might be the strongest endorsement for a program and the most effective marketing tool. This can be powerful for external programs at universities, workforce development programs at community colleges, corporate training and development, and major conferences.

HOW TO USE REACTION OBJECTIVES

Level 1 reaction objectives can be used in several ways. Although, in the eyes of some clients and sponsors, they are the least useful objectives, they still should be developed and used properly. Here are a few possibilities.

Program Design

Because most reaction questions focus directly on content, low ratings might signal that content isn't relevant, useful, practical, timely, motivational, and so forth. The designers and developers can use this information to make adjustments so that content sparks the reaction desired.

Program Delivery and Implementation

Those involved in delivering, implementing, or organizing a project or program need objectives about the planned success of the process. Some key reaction objectives focus directly on how they have organized, delivered, and supported that process. Objectives let them know how to design for the reaction that the program owner desires.

Communication to Participants

Sometimes participants need to understand the intended reaction. This keeps them aware of the collective effort of the entire team and its goals at this level. Otherwise, they might wonder what reaction was desired.

Facilitator Evaluation

Perhaps the most immediate reaction objective is the evaluation of the facilitator or team leader. In learning and development, leadership development, coaching, and process improvement, the facilitator needs feedback. The facilitator sees his or her role as ensuring that participants had a highly favorable reaction to every aspect of the project; therefore, he or she wants to know how the team reacted. For other projects where there are no formal learning and development efforts, the evaluation of the team leader might come into play. Much of the feedback goes directly to that person.

The Deceptive Feedback Cycle

There is a danger of placing too much reliance on reaction, particularly using it for facilitator evaluation. The learning and development field has a history of playing games with Level 1 objectives and data. The objective is for the participants to enjoy the program, and the facilitator is the centerpiece of that enjoyment. As shown in Figure 4.1, if participants enjoy the program, the facilitator ratings are often high (Dixon, 1990). Consequently, in many organizations, facilitators are primarily rewarded on those ratings. When that is the case, they naturally focus on creating an enjoyable experience. Certainly, nothing is wrong with enjoying the program. A certain level of enjoyment and satisfaction is an absolute must, but not at the cost of content. As some of our professional colleagues say, "We quickly migrate to the business of entertaining instead of the business of learning." To avoid this, several actions can be taken:

> Facilitators should be evaluated on Level 2 (Learning), Level 3 (Application), occasionally Level 4 (Impact), and maybe even Level 5 (ROI). This keeps a balanced perspective and prevents an overreliance on reaction objectives.
> Evaluation objectives should focus primarily on content-related issues, as described in this section. Facilitator ratings are but a small part of the experience.
> The value of Level 1 objectives has to be put into perspective. From the point of view of clients and sponsors, these data are not very valuable. In fact, many sponsors consider them essentially worthless. This is not so for other stakeholders—the designer, developer, facilitator, and participants, for example. But for the individual funding the program, reaction objectives have very little value.

Figure 4.1: The Deceptive Feedback Cycle

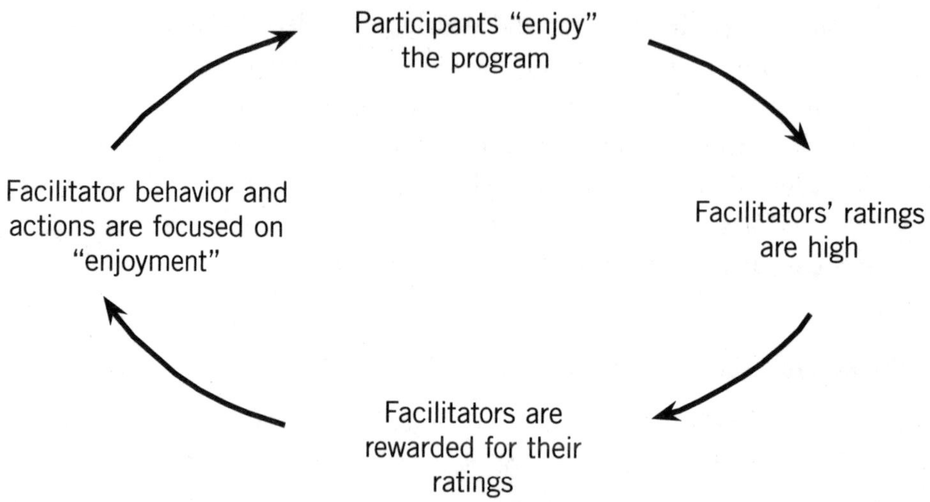

Participants "enjoy" the program

Facilitators' ratings are high

Facilitators are rewarded for their ratings

Facilitator behavior and actions are focused on "enjoyment"

EXAMPLES

Writing reaction objectives is quick and easy. The action verbs in Table 4.1 can be combined with the topics presented in Table 4.4 to present simple reaction measures. Additional precision can be offered with desired ratings or the percentage rating "yes" compared to "no." Scales from 1 to 10 or even zero to 100 have been used to judge the reaction; however, 5-point and 7-point scales are most often used as they provide sufficient variance in scoring for this type of measurement.

Examples of reaction objectives from one project are presented in Table 4.5. These are the reaction objectives taken from an annual conference of insurance agents. In this situation, the program designer desired very specific reactions and set the objectives indicated in the table (Phillips, Myhill, & McDonough, 2007).

FINAL THOUGHTS

In this chapter we've outlined the steps to develop reaction objectives—a simple process. Often understood, but not specifically written or communicated,

Table 4.5: Reaction Objectives for an Annual Insurance Agents Conference

At the end of the conference, participants should rate each of the following statements 4 out of 5 on a 5-point scale:

> The meeting was organized.

> The speakers were effective.

> The meeting was valuable for business development.

> The meeting content was important to my success.

> The meeting was motivational for me personally.

> The meeting had practical content.

> The meeting contained new information.

> The meeting represented an excellent use of my time.

> I will use the material from this conference.

these objectives are far more effective if clearly spelled out for all parties. Reaction is important, as a negative reaction can doom a project to failure. Reaction objectives pinpoint the areas critical to project success. This chapter details how these objectives are developed and presents 27 possible areas to evaluate. Taken in its total, this is far too many. The critical challenge is to select only the measures most important to the project, providing the information that the various stakeholders need. Then the data must be used to make adjustments and changes, but not be overemphasized. These data, after all, are perceived as less valuable in the eyes of many program owners and sponsors. Relying on it as the key measure for facilitators, for example, might result in placing too much emphasis on the enjoyable part of the program and not enough on the content. The next chapter focuses on a higher level of objectives, learning objectives.

EXERCISE: WHAT'S WRONG WITH THESE REACTION OBJECTIVES?

Examine the objectives in Table 4.6. Under each objective, indicate what is wrong with the objective. Responses to this exercise are provided in Appendix A.

Table 4.6: What's Wrong With These Reaction Objectives?

1. Participants should like this program.

2. The conference content will be understood by all attendees.

3. Overall, participants should be satisfied at the end of the project.

4. Participants should rate this workshop very stimulating as indicated by a rating of 4 on a 5-point scale.

5. Participants should find that the content of this program is not too difficult.

Learning Objectives

When contrasted with the two levels of objectives previously discussed (Input and Reaction), Level 2 (Learning) objectives need to be more precise and performance driven. This chapter shows typical ways in which learning objectives are developed and used to evaluate skills and knowledge acquisition.

ARE LEARNING OBJECTIVES NECESSARY?

As we move up the chain of impact, the objectives become more important. Few would disagree that learning objectives are more important than having clearly defined input and reaction objectives. While they are all important, learning objectives define what individuals must know to succeed with a project or program. In some programs, such as learning and development, competency building, technology implementation, and leadership development, learning is a critical part of the process—perhaps the most important part. The best learning objectives are those that capture in specific terms what participants must know to be successful.

For compliance programs, where the definition of compliance is based on individuals' knowledge, a learning objective becomes the most crucial measure. For these programs, learning objectives might be the highest level of objective pursued.

For projects or programs where learning is not as significant, learning and knowledge are still necessary for project implementation success; therefore, learning objectives are required. While all solutions are not learning solutions, all solutions include a learning component. For example, consider an exhibitor at a major conference. The exhibitor uses a booth or display to communicate to current and prospective clients. The ultimate success of the exhibit is usually judged by additional sales or new clients—impact objectives (Level 4). Some would argue that learning is not an issue in this situation and that learning objectives would not be appropriate; however, all levels are in play in this scenario. For example, the exhibitor wants clients to have certain reactions as they approach the exhibit, peruse the information, and discuss products and services with client representatives. The exhibitor wants clients to know about the company, the brand, the message, and the products and services so they can take appropriate steps to make a purchase. Knowledge is critical. Moving on to Level 3, the exhibitor wants clients to follow up with action, such as checking out a product, visiting the website, ordering more informational materials, reviewing a sample, participating in a demonstration, or having a salesperson call. All of these are application objectives, which lead to impact objectives of driving sales. But to be successful in meeting application and impact objectives, the exhibitor realizes that potential clients must first know what the company offers.

HOW TO CONSTRUCT LEARNING OBJECTIVES

Learning objectives require more precision than input and reaction objectives. The best learning objectives are clearly written with action verbs and are performance focused. They might contain conditions and criteria (Mager, 1984).

Action Verbs

Learning objectives usually contain action verbs and are performance based. Specific action verbs reduce the risk of misinterpretation. For example, if a new strategy is being launched and it is expected that participants understand the strategy, an objective might read, "After completion of this session, participants should understand the strategy." However, this objective is nonspecific and can lead to misinterpretation. The definition of *understand* is vague. A more precise objective would be, "After completing this session, participants should identify the five elements of the strategy and name the three pillars of the strategy." These verbs identify action and leave no doubt as to the objective's meaning. Table 5.1 lists typical specific verbs used in objectives.

Words to avoid are those without clear meaning, such as *know, understand, internalize,* and *appreciate.* These words are open to interpretation and should be avoided in learning objectives. This is not to suggest that if a learning objective uses the word *understand* that it is absolutely wrong. However, it probably is not the best choice to convey meaning, and it opens the door to challenges when time to measure success.

Performance

Essentially, performance describes what the participant will be able to do after participating or becoming involved in a project or program. To be precise, learning objectives must state what the participants will be able to do based on observable (visual or audible) behavior. The key question to ask is what a person will be doing to demonstrate mastery of the particular objective. This leads to the precise action verbs listed in Table 5.1. Consider this example: "Given the detailed client information, write a proposal for the product that meets the client's needs." This statement is performance driven, as the participant must produce a proposal, which is a visible action.

The issue of overt and covert objectives is important when addressing performance. An overt objective clearly expresses an action item that can be observed or heard, such as the example above. In a covert objective, the action

Table 5.1: Action Verbs for Objectives

➤ Name	➤ Explain	➤ Complete
➤ Write	➤ Search	➤ State
➤ Prepare	➤ Sort	➤ Build
➤ Describe	➤ Locate	➤ Start up
➤ Recite	➤ Stop	➤ List
➤ Reboot	➤ Solve	➤ Compare
➤ Differentiate	➤ Calculate	➤ Recall
➤ Identify	➤ Eliminate	➤ Contrast
➤ Load	➤ Construct	➤ Discontinue

is internalized, but lacks observable action. For example, in the objective, "Contrast the differences between consumer and commercial loans," the individual could make the contrast mentally, which would not be visible. This is a covert objective. To make a covert objective more usable, a statement is often added to provide a way to make the objective more observable. For example, the above objective could be rewritten as, "Contrast the differences between consumer and commercial loans, and write the key differences." The action of writing provides an overt measurement.

Conditions

When writing a learning objective, following the performance/action verb approach above is a step toward well-developed learning objectives; however, more detail might be necessary. Sometimes the parameters or conditions under which a person is expected to perform might need to be detailed. For example, consider the objective, "At the end of the conference, write a business development plan." The question of condition comes into play here. Are participants supposed to write the plan from memory, or will guidelines or templates be provided? We suspect some example or guideline will be offered. So the new objective could be, "At the end of the conference, write a business development plan using the template supplied by the facilitator." The revised objective gives more detail on the conditions under which the performance should occur.

Conditions can be written in a variety of ways. Table 5.2 shows the typical conditions for learning objectives. They provide additional detail to define what is expected. For example, instead of having an objective to calculate ROI for a technology project, the objective might be reworded as, "Given the total monetary benefits of the project and the total cost of the project, calculate the ROI." In this statement, detail helps communicate expectations. The amount of detail should be adequate for participants to understand clearly what they must do. It must also be clear to any other stakeholder involved.

Criterion

In addition to action verbs and detailed conditions, a third dimension is helpful in developing learning objectives: stating clearly how well something is to be done. For example, an objective is, "Be able to list eight out of 10 elements of the company's sexual harassment policy, given a copy of the policy." The objective is met when eight out of 10 of the policy items are listed, given the policy. The eight out of 10 is the expected level of performance or the criterion for success.

Table 5.2: Typical Conditions for Learning Objectives

> Given the attached job aid . . .

> Given a list of . . .

> Given any reference of the participant's choice . . .

> Using a template . . .

> Given a sample size table . . .

> When provided with a standard set of tools . . .

> Given a properly functioning laptop . . .

> Without the aid of references . . .

> Without the aid of a calculator . . .

> With the aid of software . . .

Adapted from *Preparing Instructional Objectives* (rev. 2nd ed.). Robert F. Mager. California: Lake Publishing Company, 1984.

Criteria can be developed by making use of speed, accuracy, and quality. An example of an accuracy criterion is in the above objective about a company's sexual harassment policy. This objective focuses on accuracy. We are allowing only two mistakes. Accuracy can be stated in a variety of ways. Table 5.3 presents sample accuracy statements for learning objectives. Each of these provide a criterion that suggests how accurate the demonstration or competency must be.

Speed reflects the desired time required to demonstrate a particular performance. For example, consider the objective, "Be able to classify the type of customer complaint in five minutes, given the complete customer complaint report." The five-minute timeframe places a speed criterion on the objective.

The third type of criterion is quality. When speed and accuracy are not the critical criteria, a quality measure might be needed. Quality focuses on waste, errors, rework, and acceptable standards. For example, in the objective, "Be able to operate the machine with no more than 2 percent waste," the percentage of waste allowed is a quality measure. Quality is similar to accuracy, but the two criteria have distinct differences. Consider the objective, "Be able to make 85 percent of the daily sales calls with success ratings of 4.8 or higher from clients." The 85 percent represents accuracy, while the success ratings reflect the quality of the sales calls.

Table 5.3: Accuracy Statements for Learning Objectives

> ➤ . . . with no more than 20% incorrect classifications.

> ➤ . . . and solutions must be accurate to the nearest two decimal places.

> ➤ . . . with materials weighed accurately to the nearest gram.

> ➤ . . . correct to at least three significant figures.

> ➤ . . . with no more than two incorrect entries for every 10 pages of the log.

> ➤ . . . with the listening accurate enough so that no more than one request for repeated information is made for each customer contact.

Adapted from *Preparing Instructional Objectives* (rev. 2nd ed.). Robert F. Mager. California: Lake Publishing Company, 1984.

Tips

Learning objectives provide a focus for participants, indicating what they must learn and do—sometimes with precision. Developing learning objectives is straightforward. The key issues are presented in Table 5.4.

CATEGORIES FOR LEARNING OBJECTIVES

There are several ways to categorize learning objectives. Although they generally focus on skills and knowledge, there are other elements that can be important. Typically, the objectives are broad and only indicate specific major skills or knowledge areas that should be achieved as the program is implemented. These are sometimes called key learning objectives. As shown in Figure 5.1, these objectives break down into subcomponents. Each key objective may have sub-objectives that provide more detail. If necessary, these sub-objectives are broken into supporting objectives and, even further, sub-supporting objectives. This is necessary when many tasks, procedures, and new skills must be learned to make the programs successful. For short programs in which the focus on learning is light, this level of detail might not be needed. Identifying the major objectives and indicating what must be accomplished to meet those objectives are often sufficient.

Table 5.4: Developing Learning Objectives

Learning objectives are critical to measuring learning because they

> communicate expected outcomes from learning

> describe competent performance that should be the result of learning

> provide a basis for evaluating learning

> focus on learning for participants.

The best learning objectives

> describe behaviors or actions that are observable and measurable

> are outcome based, clearly worded, and specific

> specify what the participant must do as a result of the program

> have three components:

  • performance—what the participant will be able to do during and after the program

  • condition—circumstances under which the participant will perform the task

  • criterion—degree, amount, or level of accuracy, quality, or time necessary to perform the task.

Three types of learning objectives are

> awareness—familiarity with terms, concepts, and processes

> knowledge—general understanding of concepts and processes

> performance—ability to demonstrate a skill or task, at least at a basic level.

Typical Measurement Categories

Learning measures focus on knowledge, skills, and attitudes, as well as confidence to apply or implement the program or process as desired. Sometimes, learning measures are expanded to different categories. Table 5.5 shows the typical measures collected at this level. Obviously, the more detailed the skills, the

Figure 5.1: A Breakdown of Objectives

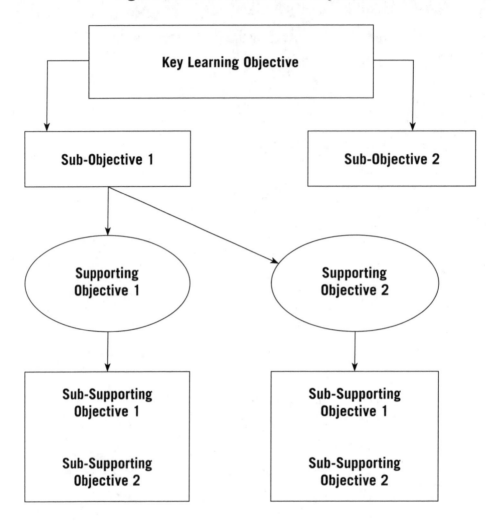

greater the number of objectives. Programs can vary, ranging from one or two simple skills to massive programs that may involve hundreds of skills.

Knowledge often includes the assimilation of facts, figures, and concepts. Instead of knowledge, the terms *awareness, understanding,* or *information* may be specific categories. Sometimes, perceptions or attitudes may change based on what a participant has learned. For example, in a diversity program, the participants' attitudes toward having a diverse work group are often changed with the implementation of the program. Sometimes, the desire is to develop a reservoir of knowledge and skills and tap into it when developing capability, capacity, or readiness. When individuals are capable, they are often described as being job ready.

Table 5.5: Typical Learning Measurement Categories		
➤ Skills	➤ Information	➤ Capacity
➤ Knowledge	➤ Perception	➤ Readiness
➤ Awareness	➤ Attitudes	➤ Confidence
➤ Understanding	➤ Capability	➤ Contracts

When participants use skills for the first time, an appropriate measure might be the confidence that the participants have to use those skills in their job settings. This becomes critical in job situations in which skills must be performed accurately and within a certain standard. Sometimes, networking is part of a program, and developing contacts that may be valuable later is important. This may be within, or external to, an organization. For example, a leadership development program may include participants from different functional parts of the organization, and an expected outcome, from a learning perspective, is to know who to contact at particular times in the future.

Cognitive Levels of Bloom's Taxonomy

Benjamin Bloom and other psychologists created a system for describing, in detail, different levels of cognitive functioning so that the precision of testing cognitive performance could be improved (Bloom, 1956). The result of this effort was a classification system that breaks cognitive processes into six types: knowledge, comprehension, application, analysis, synthesis, and evaluation. The scheme is called a taxonomy, because each level is subsumed by the next, higher level. Since its creation, the taxonomy has been widely used to classify the cognitive level of learning objectives.

> ➤ The *knowledge* level is the lowest level of the taxonomy and simply indicates the ability to remember content in exactly the same form in which it was presented.
> ➤ The *comprehension* level consists of one of the following:

> Participants restate material in their own words.
> Participants translate information from one form to another.
> Participants apply designated rules.
> Participants recognize previously unseen examples of concepts.

> The *application* level requires participants to decide what rules are pertinent to a given problem and then to apply the rules to solve the problem. Although the term *application* is used, it is still a learning objective.
> At the *analysis* level, participants are required to break complex situations into their component parts and figure out how the parts relate to and influence one another.
> The *synthesis* level requires the creation of totally original material: products, designs, equipment, and so forth.
> The *evaluation* level is the highest level of Bloom's taxonomy. This level requires participants to judge the appropriateness or value of some object, plan, design, and so on, for some purpose (Shrock & Coscarelli, 2000).

For most projects or programs, these levels of learning might not be necessary. For significant learning solutions, however, it might be helpful to classify objectives by these categories.

HOW TO USE LEARNING OBJECTIVES

Learning objectives are highly useful, giving projects proper direction and guidance. Here are five important uses.

Program Design

Learning objectives give specific direction to the designers. Using the objectives, designers build the appropriate content into the exercises, skill practice tests, and assessments.

Program Facilitation

Learning objectives give proper direction to facilitators by helping them understand what they must teach. For project leaders, these objectives show what participants and others involved in the project must know to make the project successful. They receive direction and guidance to ensure that the knowledge and skills are acquired by participants.

Marketing

Learning objectives are often important in marketing a project or program. They show what participants will learn to implement the project or program and make it successful. Detailed learning objectives might attract additional participants.

Participant Confidence

Learning objectives are fundamental information for participants. Before, during, and after the project or program, the objectives remind participants of what they should learn to make the program successful. These objectives provide clear direction of what is needed and perhaps the motivation to learn some of the material in advance of the program initiation.

Compliance

Sometimes learning objectives are used for compliance purposes. They show what must occur to meet a mandatory compliance or regulatory requirement. In these cases, objectives align with the requirements. When the objectives are met, the requirements are satisfied.

EXAMPLES

Table 5.6 shows some typical learning objectives. These objectives are critical to measuring learning. They communicate the expected outcomes of learning and define the desired competence or performance necessary for program success.

Table 5.6: Typical Learning Objectives

After completing the program, participants will be able to

> identify the six features of the new ethics policy
> demonstrate the use of each software routine in the standard time for the routine
> use problem-solving skills, given a specific problem statement
> determine whether they are eligible for the early retirement program
> score 75 or better in 10 minutes on the new-product quiz
> demonstrate all five customer-interaction skills with a success rating of 4 out of a possible 5
> explain the five categories for the value of diversity in a work group
> document suggestions for award consideration
> score at least 9 out of 10 on a sexual harassment policy quiz
> identify five new technology trends explained at the conference
> name the six pillars of the division's new strategy
> successfully complete the leadership simulation in 15 minutes.

Table 5.7 shows the actual objectives taken from an annual agents conference organized by an insurance company. As you can see, it specifically indicates what the agents must learn at the conference (Phillips, Myhill, & McDonough, 2007).

Table 5.7: Examples of Learning Objectives From an Annual Agents Conference

After completing the conference, participants should be able to

> identify the five steps for business development strategy

> develop a business development plan, given a template

> select the best community service group to join for business development

> explain the changes in products within 10 minutes

> identify the five most effective ways to turn a contact into a sale

> identify at least five agents to call for suggestions and advice.

Adapted from "Neighborhood Insurance Company Case Study," *Proving the Value of Meetings and Events.* J.J. Phillips, M. Myhill, & J. McDonough. Birmingham, Alabama: ROI Institute and MPI, 2007.

FINAL THOUGHTS

Learning objectives, representing the second level of success in the chain of impact, are more involved than input and reaction objectives, as they must be clearly stated to prevent misinterpretation. Ideally, they should include an action verb, a performance statement, a condition, and a criterion. Not every objective should have all these elements, but these are the components necessary to make a comprehensive learning objective. For projects and programs where the learning component is prominent, learning objectives become extremely critical and must be developed with precision. When they are defined clearly, they provide direction for groups to build content and understand what is necessary to make the project successful. Chapter 6 will focus on the next level of objectives, application objectives.

EXERCISE: WHAT'S WRONG WITH THESE LEARNING OBJECTIVES?

Table 5.8 presents a list of learning objectives that need improvement. Indicate the concerns about the objectives, as stated. Responses to this exercise are provided in Appendix A.

Table 5.8: What's Wrong With These Learning Objectives?

1. Given a one-hour session, be able to understand the difference among rebate, adjustment, and fee waiver.

2. The participant will learn basic construction standards in the home-building industry, according to local and state codes.

3. Understand the principles of leadership.

4. Be able to recognize that the implementation of a great place to work requires time, adjustment, and continuous effort.

5. Appreciate the viewpoint of others and perform as a great teammate.

6. Demonstrate knowledge of the principles of project management.

7. Be able to know well the major rules of SPIN selling.

8. Be able to develop logical approaches to the solution of network downtime.

CHAPTER 6

Application Objectives

This chapter pushes the objective chain of impact to the next level, Level 3 (Application). With examples and exercises, the chapter presents techniques for developing performance-based application objectives. Objectives at this level define the actions participants will take after the program is conducted or the project is implemented. This is an uncomfortable level for some professionals, as they might have less control over success in achieving these objectives. Typical issues in developing application objectives are addressed in this chapter, along with tips on how to use them in the most effective way.

ARE APPLICATION OBJECTIVES NECESSARY?

Most program leaders would argue that the development and use of application objectives are absolutely necessary. After all, these objectives provide direction to participants and clarify expectations in their own work or life situation. They create the expectation of what will be accomplished within a desired timeframe. However, others might take the stance that application objectives are not needed. This view comes from two assumptions. First, when Level 2 (Learning) objectives are clearly developed and participants master what is needed for program success, it is assumed that they will perform in a way that reflects what they have learned. Second, program facilitators or leaders have no influence on participants after they leave the program or project. Therefore, there is no control over these individuals, rendering application objectives inappropriate or ineffective.

These two assumptions are not necessarily accurate in practice. First, participants do not always do what they have learned to do when a project is implemented. This is woefully apparent in the learning and development field, where 60–90 percent of what individuals learn in formal learning programs is not used on the job. Many barriers interfere with successful application of almost every program. To drive (or at least influence) application, objectives must be established and communicated to participants, their supervisors, and others involved in the learning process. To apply what was learned properly, participants need clear expectations about what they must do. For example, consider learning new software. In a classroom environment, participants might learn all the routines for the software. In reality, though, they need only learn parts of it to succeed on the job. The application objective defines how and when they will likely use the software on the job. Project or program objectives set expectations for participants' supervisors so they can give proper support.

The second assumption—that program facilitators and team leaders have no influence on participants in their own job environment—is inaccurate in today's workplace. Objectives are developed for the entire project or program, not simply for the learning sessions or early stages of the initiative. While it is true that a facilitator or team leader can have more control over learning objectives during the program and less control over application objectives, he or she can still influence success with application objectives. With application objectives, the facilitator teaches with application in mind, using the work environment as the context. Using personal experience, the facilitator examines barriers and shows how to minimize or overcome them. He or she creates expectations and shows participants how it's done.

At various times, different stakeholders have more or less influence on a particular objective. As a result, the application objectives become an important extension of the learning objectives. They provide direction and guidance, as well as form the basis for evaluation.

HOW TO CONSTRUCT APPLICATION OBJECTIVES

The good news is that the development of application objectives essentially mirrors the development of learning objectives. Learning objectives define what participants must learn, while application objectives define what participants are expected to do with what they have learned.

Application objectives have their own distinct areas of emphasis. First, they should include an action verb that has clear meaning. (Refer to the verbs listed in Table 5.1 in the previous chapter.) Second, a performance requirement is connected to the action verb. The performance element is clear, as in Level 2 (Learning) objectives. The statement might be as simple as completing a report or making a phone call or as complex as using a comprehensive skill or completing a detailed action plan.

Third, conditions can still exist, but they might not be readily apparent. For example, in a learning session, participants are given requirements or a reference and then are asked to demonstrate knowledge. In the job setting, the given requirements are sometimes already on the job and are understood; therefore, the objective might not always include the given condition.

Fourth, criterion becomes more important in a follow-up evaluation. The criterion—whether speed, accuracy, or quality—is needed because the importance of success with these criteria is critical. Most application objectives include a time limit, which is sometimes assumed to be understood. For example, participants learn a particular skill and are expected to apply that skill three weeks later. Having an objective to use the skill without the time-frame might still suggest a three-week period. To be more specific and ensure participants are clear about this expectation, however, the time should be identified in each objective. Take accuracy as another example. Participants might be required to complete 80 percent of their action items by a certain date. Quality is also important. The application might indicate that a skill or task must be completed with less than a 1 percent error rate or with a minimal success rating from an observer.

Application objectives are critical because they describe the intermediate outputs—outputs occurring between the learning of new tasks and procedures and the impact that this learning will deliver. Application and implementation objectives describe how things should be or the state of the workplace after the program is implemented. They provide a basis for the evaluation of on-the-job changes and performance. They emphasize what has occurred on the job as a result of the program.

Table 6.1 shows the key issues involved in developing application objectives. Application objectives have almost always been included to some degree in programs or projects, but have not always been as specific as they could be or need to be. To be effective, they must clearly define the expected environment in the workplace following the successful program implementation.

Table 6.1: Developing Application Objectives

The best application objectives

> identify behaviors, tasks, and actions that are observable and measurable

> are outcome based, clearly worded, and specific

> specify what the participant will change, or has changed, as a result of the program or project

> may have three components:

  • performance—what the participant has changed or accomplished at a specified follow-up time

  • condition—circumstances under which the participant performed the task, procedures, or action

  • criterion—degree or level of accuracy, quality, or time within which the task or job is performed.

Key questions:

> What new or improved *knowledge* was applied to the job?

> What new or improved *skill* was applied to the job?

> What is the *frequency of skill* application?

> What new *tasks* will be performed?

> What new *steps* will be implemented?

> What new *action items* will be implemented?

> What new *procedures* will be implemented or changed?

> What new *guidelines* will be implemented or changed?

> What new *processes* will be implemented or changed?

The detail on developing application objectives is referred to in the previous material in chapter 5, addressing learning objectives. The basis is the same (action verb, performance statement, a condition, and a criterion). With application objectives, however, the criterion becomes more important, and the conditions become less important.

TOPICS FOR APPLICATION OBJECTIVES

The topics addressed at this level parallel many of those identified in chapters 4 and 5. Therefore, many of the areas detailed in those chapters can be mapped into this level. For example, questions about the intent to apply what is learned in the program are logical issues to measure at this time—when the application and implementation occur. However, because of the timing for successful application, additional opportunities to measure success arise.

Objectives at this level focus on activity or action, not the consequences of those actions (which is Level 4, Impact). The number of activities to measure at this level can be mindboggling. Table 6.2 shows some coverage areas for application objectives. While the examples can vary, the action items shown are included in many projects and programs.

HOW TO USE APPLICATION OBJECTIVES

Application objectives are developed when the program is conceived, based on the initial analysis detailed in chapter 2. When this takes place, it occurs before the project or program is designed, developed, and delivered. For that reason, application objectives have powerful consequences. Here is a sample of uses.

Program Design

Application objectives provide guidance to the designers, showing them how they must position the content with an eye on application. The exercises, skill practices, and role plays, which are part of any learning session connected to a project, are now job related. They're more realistic in that they have scenarios and situations that reflect the work conditions.

Program Facilitation

Application objectives are provided to those who teach learning and development sessions, provide on-the-job coaching, or coordinate a project team for implementation of software. The objectives essentially define what will occur as the skills and knowledge are used, the task is completed, or the software or procedure is installed. They take the mystery out of what must be accomplished. When the objectives are in place, the facilitators teach to the test. The test is now on-the-job application. The facilitators and team leaders bring their own experience to the situation so that they see clearly how to manage the use of the content and the implementation of the project material.

Table 6.2: Examples of Coverage Areas for Application

Action	Explanation	Example
Increase	Increase a particular activity or action.	Increase the frequency of the use of a particular skill.
Decrease	Decrease a particular activity or action.	Decrease the number of times a particular process has to be checked.
Eliminate	Stop or remove a particular task or activity.	Eliminate the formal follow-up meeting and replace it with a virtual meeting.
Maintain	Keep the same level of activity for a particular process.	Continue to monitor the process with the same schedule as previously used.
Create	Design, build, or implement a new procedure, process, or activity.	Create a procedure for resolving the differences between two divisions.
Use	Use a particular process or activity.	Use the new skill in situations for which it was designed to be used.
Perform	Conduct or do a particular task or procedure.	Perform a post-audit review at the end of each activity.
Participate	Become involved in various activities, projects, or programs.	Each associate should submit a suggestion for reducing costs.
Enroll	Sign up for a particular process, program, or project.	Each associate should enroll in the career advancement program.
Respond	React to groups, individuals, or systems.	Each participant in the program should respond to customer inquiries within 15 minutes.
Network	Facilitate relationships with others who are involved or have been affected by the program.	Each program participant should continue networking with contacts on at least a quarterly basis.

Participants

Application objectives are provided to participants, who need direction and clearly defined expectations. These objectives define how participants should perform on the job as a result of the project or program. They take the mystery out of what participants must do. Too often, participants who might learn specific content in a formal session are left wondering, "How much of this will I have to do? Will I use part or any of this? Does this apply to me?" Detailed application objectives answer these questions.

Managers of Participants

Sometimes application objectives are provided to managers of participants. This important group can influence on-the-job performance more than any other stakeholder group. Managers have a huge impact on what the participants do and how they spend their time. Application objectives provide clear direction for these managers. They show them what the participants must do to make the process work. Also, the objectives sometimes provide information that will help managers support and reinforce the performance profile.

Evaluators

For evaluators, Level 3 objectives provide clear direction. They not only indicate specific measures to be sought, but in some cases they provide hints as to the source or location of the data and when the data should be collected. The evaluator's job is much easier. Application objectives often map directly into action plans or questionnaires so that follow-up information can be readily obtained. This saves time for evaluators who struggle to have the resources needed to conduct their evaluations.

EXAMPLES

As a program is implemented, the application objectives clearly define what is expected and often to what level of performance. Application objectives are similar to learning objectives, but reflect actual use on the job. They also might involve specific milestones, indicating when part or all of the process is implemented. Table 6.3 shows typical application objectives.

Table 6.4 presents the application objectives for an annual agents conference. These objectives mirror the learning objectives presented in the same case study in the previous chapter. They provide the direction, guidance, and expectations for all parties involved. Table 6.5 shows the objectives for a

Table 6.3: Typical Application Objectives

When the program is implemented

> at least 99.1 percent of software users will be following the correct sequences after three weeks of use

> within one year, 10 percent of employees will submit documented suggestions for saving costs

> the average 360-degree leadership assessment score will improve from 3.4 to 4.1 on a 5-point scale in 90 days

> 95 percent of high-potential employees will complete all steps in their individual development plans within two years

> employees will routinely use problem-solving skills when faced with a quality problem

> sexual harassment activity will cease within three months after the zero-tolerance policy is implemented

> 80 percent of employees will use one or more of the three cost-containment features of the health-care plan in the next six months

> 50 percent of conference attendees will follow up with at least one contact from the conference within 60 days

> by November, pharmaceutical sales reps will communicate adverse effects of a specific prescription drug to all physicians in their territories

> managers will initiate three workout projects within 15 days

> sales and customer service representatives will use all five interaction skills with at least half the customers within the next month.

leadership development program. Although some of the objectives are not as precise as they could be, they clearly show what is expected of the individual and, for the most part, under what criterion.

FINAL THOUGHTS

This chapter shows how to develop application objectives, those that position the use of the program or project content relative to the job. These objectives are developed essentially the same as learning objectives but in an on-the-job

Table 6.4: Application Objectives From an Annual Agents Conference

After the conference is completed, participants will

> implement a business development plan within three weeks and report results in three months

> use two new business development strategies within three months

> contact at least 10 percent of the current customer base to offer new changes in auto insurance coverage within three months

> make a random 5 percent customer service check with current clients within six months.

> in 30 days, follow up with at least three agents to discuss successes, concerns, or issues

> within three weeks, join at least one additional community service group targeted for a potential customer base

> use selling skills daily.

Adapted from *Proving the Value of Meetings and Events.* J.J. Phillips, M. Myhill, & J. McDonough. Birmingham, Alabama: ROI Institute and MPI, 2007.

context. The chapter shows many examples of properly constructed application objectives and emphasized the power of these higher levels of objectives to provide direction and guidance to a variety of stakeholders. The next chapter presents the next level of objectives—those representing impact.

EXERCISE: WHAT'S WRONG WITH THESE APPLICATION OBJECTIVES?

In developing objectives, it is useful to examine some objectives that have issues. Table 6.6 shows a list of less-than-perfect objectives. For each objective, indicate the issue or problem. Responses to this exercise are provided in Appendix A.

Table 6.5: Application Objectives From a Leadership Development Program

After the program is implemented, participants will

> apply the 11-step goal-setting process for the team within three months

> install the 12-step leadership planning process in three weeks

> routinely use the 12 core competencies of outstanding leaders

> identify 10 ways to create higher levels of employee loyalty and report them to their managers within 30 days

> use the concept of Deferred Judgment in five scenarios within three months

> use the creative problem-solving process within an identified problem

> use five of the seven best ways to build positive relationships in 30 days

> given an unacceptable work situation, apply the four-step approach to address ineffective work habits

> each week, practice the six ways to improve communication effectiveness.

Table 6.6: What's Wrong With These Application Objectives?

1. Apply leadership skills.

2. After completing this program, participants will have a better understanding of the new corporate diversity policy.

3. Three months after the program, participants will successfully complete a project management simulation exercise.

4. Participants will communicate much better.

5. Sixty days after the program is completed, the participants will rate the program as valuable.

6. Three months after the supervisor's participation in the program, employees will rate the supervisor as an effective leader.

7. During the program, participants will successfully use a customer-complaint process with a live customer complaining about a product.

8. After this program, participants will stop attending unnecessary meetings.

CHAPTER 7

Impact Objectives

For some stakeholders, impact objectives are the most important. These objectives represent both tangible and intangible measures. This chapter focuses on developing Level 4 (Impact) objectives. These objectives are based on business measures that are plentiful throughout organizations. Data developed at Level 4 are explored, along with the issues involved in writing the objectives. The development of these objectives is straightforward. Several examples are presented.

ARE IMPACT OBJECTIVES NECESSARY?

The chain of impact presented in chapter 1 presents the impact objectives as the consequence of a program or project. These objectives are reflected in measures of hard data, such as output, quality, cost, and time, as well as soft data, such as customer satisfaction, employee engagement, and brand awareness. These objectives are particularly important for senior executives. Some executives lack enthusiasm about a project or program unless the results reflect key business measures. These impact measures are found in operating reports, scorecards, dashboards, and key performance indicators. It is often the deficiency in performance of one or more impact measures that has led to the creation of the program. This was discussed in chapter 2. In terms of power to affect project design, delivery, and success, impact objectives are the most powerful. They provide the focus needed to drive the results that top executives desire.

In practice, many programs do not contain these impact objectives. This is particularly true in soft programs, such as learning and development, human resources, leadership development, executive coaching, communication, change management, public relations, and compliance. In reality, each of these types of programs can be connected to a business measure and thus have business impact objectives connected to them. The challenge is to perform the analysis described in chapter 2 and develop the objectives using the techniques in this chapter.

HOW TO CONSTRUCT IMPACT OBJECTIVES

Chapter 2 focused on how objectives are developed working through levels of needs assessment. A business measure reflects a business need. Job performance needs and the subsequent analysis ensure that the business measure is connected to the project or program. When this happens, the business need is clearly defined and is the primary driver in selecting or developing the program or project.

Precise Definition

It is important to ensure that the precise definition of the impact measure is offered. Definitions can vary considerably. For example, a broad definition of quality is unusable. Quality may be defined as errors, rework, warranty claims, or low scores on industry-wide customer satisfaction surveys. The specific quality measure must be defined, which occurs during the business needs analysis. Consider employee turnover. An objective for a project might be to reduce employee turnover. The wording here is too vague, however, and needs to be defined as involuntary turnover, avoidable turnover, or regrettable turnover. The definitions are critical so that the specific measure becomes a focus during the project or program.

A Consequence of Action

A business impact measure, the basis for the impact objective, is a consequence of a specific action. In chapter 2, the initial analysis included a step to determine what participants are doing or not doing on the job that is influencing the business measure. This translates into the specific action needed and is written as an application objective. Sometimes, there is confusion between Levels 3 and 4. Level 3 (Application) is always action (activity), and Level 4 (Impact) is the consequence of that action. Consider the objective to reduce project management time by 20 percent. Some may consider this a Level 3 objective, in which participants will simply reduce the amount of time. However, to accomplish the objective, participants must do something different. What has worked before is not working. Perhaps a new process, policy, tool, or even training is needed to manage the project. Any of these solutions can reduce time if implemented properly. The Level 3 objective would be the use of the process, policy, tool, or training. The time reduction is the consequence of the use of the process, policy, tool, or training (that is, reduction in time)— a Level 4 objective. This distinction should be reviewed constantly to ensure understanding of these two types of objectives.

Criterion

As with learning and application objectives, impact objectives should include a criterion. The criterion is usually defined as speed, accuracy, or quality and follows the same rules stated in chapters 5 and 6. For example, an objective for a safety project might be that government-imposed safety fines should decrease from $2.5 million per year to less than $500,000 within one year after project completion. This objective includes accuracy and time criteria. This degree of specificity is needed to measure success. For some projects, the specificity is at the individual level. For example, a project designed to increase sales in a new-product launch could vary with each individual customer relationship manager. In some territories, the new product has little competition, and the growth number can be set high. In others, where competition is intense, the growth number might be much smaller. In this circumstance, an overall objective might be more appropriate. For example, the objective might be that sales reach a 12 percent increase throughout the entire company. The key here is to make the objective specific enough to communicate what is desired.

Successive Impact Measures

A potentially confusing issue is the fact that some impact measures have a successive chain of impact. The difficulty lies in deciding whether one objective is an appropriate measure or if all measures are objectives. For example, Table 7.1 details five possible consequences of sexual harassment in the workplace. The victim of the harassment suffers stress; the victim's job satisfaction drops; internal complaints of sexual harassment increase; the victim is increasingly

Table 7.1: Successive Impact Measures

	Level	Sexual Harassment	Data (one year)		
Stress →					
Job Satisfaction →					
	3	Sexual Harassment →		Absenteeism →	Turnover →
	4	Formal Internal Complaints →	55		
	4	External Charges →	24		
	4	Litigated Complaints →	10		
	4	Legal Fees/Expenses →	$632,000		
	4	Settlements/Losses →	$450,000		
	4	Total Cost Prevention/Investigation/Defense	$1,655,000		

Adapted from "Preventing Sexual Harassment—Healthcare Inc.," chapter 1, *Proving the Value of HR: ROI Case wStudies*. P.P. Phillips & J.J. Phillips. Birmingham, Alabama: ROI Institute and MPI, 2007.

absent from work; and employee turnover rises as victims seek employment elsewhere. The difficulty lies in determining which measures (if not all) are influenced by a sexual harassment prevention program. Most of this is sorted out in the up-front needs assessment to ensure that the particular program can indeed influence all these measures. Even if the principal focus of the program is to reduce complaints, it is important to determine whether the other measures are connected. If they are, they also could become objectives for the program.

When considering complaints, there is a successive series of Level 4 (Impact) measures. A formal internal complaint, if not resolved, could convert to an external charge with the Equal Employment Opportunity Commission. If that charge is not resolved to the victim's satisfaction, he or she has a right to sue the employer, creating a litigated complaint. Litigation leads to legal fees and expenses and also to settlements. Ultimately, all of this, from prevention to investigation to defense, represents a significant cost (Phillips & Phillips, 2007).

A program could actually have objectives for each of these. Although they should all improve in relative proportion, this might not be the case. Under U.S. law, employees have a right to sue an employer, even before an external charge is actually resolved or if it is resolved in favor of the victim. For those reasons, the focus might be on reducing the number of litigated complaints. The confusion comes when the monetary value of this program is calculated. Converting data to monetary value is critical to evaluation when an ROI calculation is developed. Using all Level 4 impact measures represents a tremendous amount of duplication. Perhaps it would be best to take one measure and use it in the conversion process. Still, they can all be objectives that are influenced by the sexual harassment prevention project. This series of successive impact measures can usually be uncovered when asking a series of "what if" questions. What if this measure happens? Does it lead to something else?

TOPICS FOR IMPACT OBJECTIVES

Impact objectives are measures located throughout the organization as common indicators. There are hundreds, if not thousands, of these measures in an organization. When identifying impact measures, consider the following issues.

Hard Versus Soft Data

To help set objectives for the desired measures, a distinction is made in two general categories of data: hard data and soft data, as described in chapter 2.

Hard data are the primary measurements of improvement, presented through rational, undisputed facts that are easily collected. They are the most desirable type of data to collect. The ultimate criteria for measuring the effectiveness of management rest on hard data items, such as productivity, profitability, cost control, and quality control. Chapter 2 provided examples of hard data grouped into categories of output, quality, cost, and time.

Hard-data measures are often supplemented with interim assessments of soft data, such as brand awareness, satisfaction, loyalty, and teamwork. Although a program designed to enhance competencies or manage change should have an ultimate impact on hard-data items, measuring soft-data items may be more efficient. While soft data may be more difficult to analyze, they are used when hard data are unavailable. Soft data are more difficult to convert to monetary values than hard data; are subjectively based, in many cases; and are less credible as a performance measurement. Chapter 2 provided a list of typical soft-data items grouped into typical categories.

The preference of hard data in programs does not minimize the value of soft data. Soft data are essential for a complete evaluation of a program; success may rest on soft-data measurements. For example, in an empowerment program at a chemical plant, three key measures of success were identified: employee stress, job satisfaction, and teamwork. All were listed as intangibles.

Most programs have objectives that use a combination of hard- and soft-data items in the evaluation. For example, a project to install new technology in a manufacturing plant had the following impact objectives:

> Reduction of production costs.
> Improvement in productivity.
> Improvement in quality.
> Reduction in inventory shortages.
> Improvement in production capability.
> Increase in technology leadership.
> Increase in job satisfaction.

These improvements included both hard data (production costs, productivity, and quality) and soft data (capability, technology, leadership, satisfaction). Most programs include both types of objectives.

Tangible Versus Intangible

The confusion about the categories of hard and soft data and the often-reduced value placed on soft data was discussed in chapter 2. This leads to a critical definition in this book. While the terms *hard data* and *soft data* can be used to discuss impact data, the terms *tangible* and *intangible* can also be used and represent a more accurate depiction. Tangible data are those data that have been converted to monetary value. Intangible data are defined as data purposely not converted to monetary value (that is, if data cannot be converted to monetary value credibly with a reasonable amount of resources, then they are reported as intangibles). This approach has several advantages. First, it avoids the sometimes confusing labels of *soft* and *hard*. Second, it negates the argument that being soft equates to little or no value. Third, it brings definition to the situation. In some organizations, a particular data item may be converted to money already, and the conversion is credible because the measure is already tangible. However, in other organizations, the same measure may not been converted and cannot be converted with a reasonable amount of resources. Therefore, it is left as intangible. Fourth, use of the terms *tangible* and *intangible* provides a rule that enhances the consistency of the evaluation process. Having such a rule helps ensure that if two people conduct the same evaluation, they will get the same or similar results.

Scorecards

Scorecards, such as those used in sporting events, provide important measures fans can review to understand the position of their team. Similar scorecards are used by top executives and often form the basis for impact objectives. In Robert Kaplan and David Norton's landmark book *The Balanced Scorecard,* this concept was brought to the attention of organizations (Kaplan & Norton, 1996). The authors suggested that data can be organized and reported from four perspectives: financial, customer, business processes, and learning and growth.

Scorecards come in a variety of types, such as Kaplan and Norton's balanced scorecard and the scorecard set in the President's Management Agenda, which uses the traffic light grading system (green for success, yellow for mixed results, red for unsatisfactory). Regardless of the type of scorecard, top executives place great emphasis on this concept. In some organizations, the scorecard concept has filtered down to various business units, and each part of the business has been required to develop scorecards.

The scorecard approach is appealing because it provides a quick comparison of key measures and examines the status of the organization. As a management tool, scorecards can be important in shaping and improving or maintaining the performance of the organization through the implementation of preventive programs. Scorecard measures often link to particular projects or programs. In many situations, a scorecard deficiency measure may have prompted the program in the first place.

Measures Linked to Specific Programs

An important issue that often surfaces when considering ROI applications is the understanding of specific measures that are often driven by specific types of programs. While there are no standard answers, Table 7.2 represents a summary of some typical measures for objectives for specific types of programs. The measures are quite broad for some programs. For example, leadership development may pay off in a variety of measures, such as improved productivity, enhanced sales and revenues, improved quality, cycle-time reduction, direct-cost savings, and employee job satisfaction. For other programs, the measures are quite narrow. Labor-management cooperation projects typically influence grievances, work stoppages, and employee satisfaction. Orientation, or onboarding, programs typically influence measures of early turnover (turnover in the first 90 days of employment), initial job performance, and initial productivity. The measures that are influenced depend on the objectives and the design of the program. Table 7.2 also illustrates the immense number of measures that can be driven or influenced.

A word of caution is needed. Presenting specific measures linked to a typical program may give the impression that these are the only measures influenced. In practice, a particular program can have many outcomes. Table 7.2 shows the most likely measures based on studies the ROI Institute has conducted or reviewed. In the course of a decade, we have been involved in more than 2,000 studies, and common threads exist among particular programs.

Relevant Measures

Existing performance measures should be thoroughly researched to identify those related to the proposed program. Several performance measures often are related to the same item. For example, the efficiency of a production unit can be measured in several ways:

> the number of units produced per hour
> the number of on-schedule production units
> the percentage of equipment used
> the percentage of equipment downtime
> the labor cost per unit of production
> the overtime required per unit of production
> total unit cost.

Table 7.2: Typical Impact Measures for Projects and Programs

Program	Key Impact Measurements
Absenteeism control/ reduction	Absenteeism, customer satisfaction, delays, job satisfaction, productivity, stress
Association meetings	Absenteeism, costs, customer service, job satisfaction, productivity, quality, sales, time, turnover
Business coaching	Costs, customer satisfaction, efficiency, employee satisfaction, productivity/output, quality, time savings
Career development/ career management	Job satisfaction, promotions, recruiting expenses, turnover
Communications programs	Conflicts, errors, job satisfaction, productivity, stress
Compensation plans	Costs, job satisfaction, productivity, quality
Compliance programs	Charges, losses, penalties/fines, settlements
Diversity	Absenteeism, charges, complaints, losses settlements, turnover
Employee retention programs	Engagement, job satisfaction, promotions, turnover
Engineering/technical/ training conferences	Costs, customer satisfaction, cycle times, downtime, job satisfaction, process time, productivity/output, quality, waste
Ethics programs	Fines, fraud, incidents, penalties, theft
E-learning	Cost savings, cycle times, error reductions, job satisfaction, productivity improvement, quality improvement,
Executive education	Absenteeism, costs, customer service, job satisfaction, productivity, quality, sales, time, turnover
Franchise/dealer meetings	Cost of sales, customer loyalty, efficiency, market share, quality, sales
Golfing events	Customer loyalty, market share, new accounts, sales, upselling
Labor-management cooperation programs	Absenteeism, grievances, job satisfaction, work stoppages
Leadership development	Cost/time savings, development, efficiency, employee satisfaction, engagement, productivity/output, quality

(continued on next page)

Table 7.2: Typical Impact Measures for Projects and Programs (continued)

Management development	Absenteeism, costs, customer service, job satisfaction, productivity, quality, sales, time, turnover
Marketing programs	Brand awareness, churn rate, cross-selling, customer loyalty, customer satisfaction, market share, new acounts, sales, upselling
Medical meetings	Compliance, efficiency, medical costs, patient satisfaction, quality
Orientation, onboarding	Early turnover, performance, productivity, quality of work, training time
Personal productivity/time management	Job satisfaction, productivity, stress reduction, time savings
Project management	Budgets, quality improvement, time savings
Quality programs	Costs, cycle times, defects, response times, rework
Retention management	Engagement, job satisfaction, turnover
Safety programs	Accident frequency rates, accident severity rates, first aid treatments
Sales training/meetings	Customer loyalty, market share, new accounts, sales
Self-directed teams	Absenteeism, customer satisfaction, job satisfaction productivity/output, quality, turnover
Sexual harassment prevention	Absenteeism, complaints, employee satisfaction, turnover
Six Sigma/lean projects	Costs, cycle times, defects, response times, rework, waste
Software projects	Absenteeism, costs, customer service, job satisfaction, productivity, quality, sales, time, turnover
Stress management	Absenteeism, job satisfaction, medical costs, turnover
Supervisor/team leader programs	Absenteeism, complaints, costs, job satisfaction, productivity, quality, sales, time, turnover
Team building	Absenteeism, costs, customer service, job satisfaction, productivity, quality, sales, time, turnover
Wellness/fitness programs	Absenteeism, accidents, medical costs, turnover

Each of these, in its own way, measures the effectiveness or efficiency of the production unit. Related measures should be reviewed to determine those most relevant to the program.

Existing Measures Converted to Usable Ones

Occasionally, existing performance measures are integrated with other data, and keeping them isolated from unrelated data may be difficult. In this situation, all existing, related measures should be extracted and tabulated again to make them more appropriate for comparison in the evaluation. At times, conversion factors may be necessary. For example, the average number of new sales orders per month may be presented regularly in the performance measures for the sales department. In addition, the sales costs per sales representative are also presented. However, in a particular program, the average cost per new sale is needed. The average number of new sales orders and the sales cost per sales representative are required to develop the data necessary for comparison.

New Measures

In a few cases, data needed to measure the success of a program are unavailable, and new data are needed. The project leader must work with the client organization to develop record-keeping systems, if economically feasible. In one organization, the sales staff's delayed responses to customer requests were an issue. This problem was discovered based on customer feedback. The feedback data prompted a project to reduce the response time. To help ensure the success of the project, several measures were planned, including measuring the actual time to respond to a customer request. Initially this measure was not available. As the program was implemented, new software was used to measure the time.

When developing new measures, several questions need to be addressed:

> Which department/section will develop the measurement system?
> Who will record and monitor the data?
> Where will it be recorded?
> Will input forms be used?
> Who will report it?

These questions will usually involve other departments or a management decision that extends beyond the scope of the project. Often the administration, operations, or technology functions will be instrumental in helping determine whether new measures are needed and, if so, how they will be developed. However, this action should be a last resort.

Summary

Developing impact objectives is relatively easy when following a few specific guidelines. Impact measures are located throughout a typical organization. The measures are there; it is a matter of connecting them to the project. Table 7.3 shows the key steps to developing impact objectives.

HOW TO USE IMPACT OBJECTIVES

Impact objectives are even more powerful than application objectives when driving results. While application objectives help remove the mystery of what

Table 7.3: Developing Business Impact Objectives

The best impact objectives

> must contain measures linked to the skills and knowledge gained as a result of the program

> describe measures that are easily collected

> represent measures that are readily available

> are results based, clearly worded, and specific

> specify what the participants have accomplished in their work or business unit as a result of the program.

Four types of impact objectives involving hard data are

> output focused

> quality focused

> cost focused

> time focused.

Three common types of impact objectives involving soft data are

> customer-service focused

> work-climate focused

> job-satisfaction focused.

participants should be doing to make the project or program successful, impact objectives show the consequence of the application, expressed in measures that are precise, meaningful, and desired by top executives. Here are a few uses for these objectives.

Program Design

Like application objectives, impact objectives give additional guidance and direction to designers and developers. Impact objectives show those who develop the content the expected ultimate outcomes. Consequently, the activities, discussions, dialogue, exercises, skill practices, and problems focus on those outcomes. Impact objectives keep the ultimate focus on why a project is being pursued. The content may change dramatically with the inclusion of impact objectives. Designers are creative people; and in the absence of specific consequences, they will fill in the blanks with perhaps incorrect information.

Program Facilitation

Impact objectives are powerful for those who lead the team. For example, in formal learning and development sessions, the facilitator has clear direction of the results of the project. Teaching will focus on the ultimate consequences, the impact measure. Here, a facilitator will use previous experience and knowledge of the measure to teach with the end result in mind. For a project team leader, the ultimate result is clearly in focus and is a goal for the team to reach—a goal that is precise, measurable, and achievable. The team's discussion will address these measures, the progress made, and the barriers that might be in the way.

Participants

Impact objectives are provided to participants so they understand how the project will benefit them personally, as well as the organization. Having an impact measure takes the mystery out of the ultimate consequence of their actions and implementation. It shows how the project will drive a particular and important measure in the organization. They see what is in it for them and what is in it for the organization. This also allows the organization to create expectations for these participants, sometimes with individual goals for the impact measure.

Marketing

Nothing sells a project or program more effectively than when impact measures are connected to the project or program. Impact objectives provide impressive information for prospective participants for routine learning and development, coaching, leadership development, team building, compliance, ethics, and even communications programs. The potential impact of the project helps to convince all interested stakeholders about the value of the project. The objectives can serve as the most important strategic marketing data possible.

Evaluators

The impact objectives guide the evaluation. The impact data sets are defined so that they are easily collected. They provide direction as to the options for isolation and data conversion. In fact, they provide the roadmap to overall success of the project or program.

EXAMPLES

Projects and programs should drive one or more business impact measures. Impact objectives represent key business measures that should be improved as the application and implementation objectives are achieved. Table 7.4 shows typical business impact objectives from a variety of projects and programs.

Table 7.4: Typical Business Impact Objectives

After completion of this program, the following conditions should be met:

> After nine months, grievances should be reduced from three per month to no more than two per month at the Golden Eagle tire plant.

> The average number of new accounts opened at Great Western Bank should increase from 300 to 350 per month in six months.

> Tardiness at the Newbury foundry should decrease by 20 percent within the next calendar year.

> There should be an across-the-board reduction in overtime for front-of-house managers at Tasty Time restaurants in the third quarter of this year.

> ❯ Employee complaints should be reduced from an average of three per month to an average of one per month at Guarantee Insurance headquarters.
>
> ❯ By the end of the year, the average number of product defects should decrease from 214 per month to 153 per month at all Amalgamated Rubber extruding plants in the Midwest region.
>
> ❯ The companywide employee engagement index should rise by one point during the next calendar year.
>
> ❯ Sales expenses for all titles at Proof Publishing Company should decrease by 10 percent in the fourth quarter.
>
> ❯ There should be a 10 percent increase in Pharmaceuticals Inc. brand awareness among physicians during the next two years.

FINAL THOUGHTS

This chapter outlines the process of developing impact objectives. Business impact objectives are critical to measuring business performance because they define the ultimate expected outcomes of the program. They describe business-unit performance that should be connected to the program. Above all, impact objectives emphasize achieving bottom-line results that key client groups expect and demand. For some, these are the most powerful objectives. They are straightforward and based on measures that are plentiful in organizations. The objectives are based on needs identified in the up-front analysis covered in chapter 2. This chapter presents additional tips and techniques to develop and fine tune impact objectives, building on the material in chapter 2. Examples were presented in this chapter, and guidelines and issues were explored. The next chapter focuses on the highest level of objectives, ROI.

EXERCISE: WHAT'S WRONG WITH THESE IMPACT OBJECTIVES?

As presented in previous chapters, problematic objectives exist. After reading Table 7.5, indicate concerns about each objective. Responses to this exercise are provided in Appendix A.

Table 7.5: What's Wrong With These Impact Objectives?

1. When this project is complete, sales will increase.

2. Increase the leadership profile of the organization.

3. Improve the capability of the organization.

4. Decrease the absenteeism and grievances in the work unit.

5. Increase the user performance profile with new SAP software.

6. Achieve a smooth implementation for Six Sigma.

7. Improve workforce effectiveness.

8. Increase the efficiency of the distribution system.

9. When this technology project is completed, it will be considered the most valuable initiative in the company's history.

CHAPTER 8

ROI Objectives

At first glance, one might wonder why we need an entire chapter to talk about ROI objectives. Isn't it merely a number? The short answer is, yes, it is a number; however, different formulas can be used to reach this number. There are specific issues that need to be addressed to use ROI appropriately.

The decision to have an ROI objective should be taken seriously. The program selected for this level of analysis should be carefully chosen. The basic premise for setting ROI objectives is that data will be collected to determine if the objectives are met. The development of ROI calculations involves important steps that go beyond what is covered in this chapter, although they are briefly mentioned. The following pages present not only the rationale for having an ROI objective, but also the ways in which it can be constructed, interpreted, and used.

ARE ROI OBJECTIVES NECESSARY?

ROI is the ultimate level of evaluation, as it compares the actual cost of a program or project to its monetary benefits. Some program sponsors demand this measure, while other stakeholders are daunted at the thought of fully exposing the program results (or lack of results). A negative ROI is always a concern.

ROI must be used carefully and reserved only for key strategic programs—important, expensive, and high-profile initiatives. To calculate ROI, the impact measures discussed in chapter 7 are converted to money and compared to program costs (using a fully loaded cost—both indirect and direct).

An ROI objective meets an important demand that is intensifying in organizations. As shown in Figure 8.1, the Show Me Evolution has occurred. Executives and key stakeholders have made higher-level demands on projects and programs, ranging from "Show me" to "Show me the real money, and make me believe it is a good investment." To achieve the latter, the process must be credible, and an ROI calculation must be made. Converting data to money and developing the fully loaded costs are beyond the scope of this book. Many other books show how this is accomplished (Phillips & Phillips, 2007; Phillips & Zuniga, 2008).

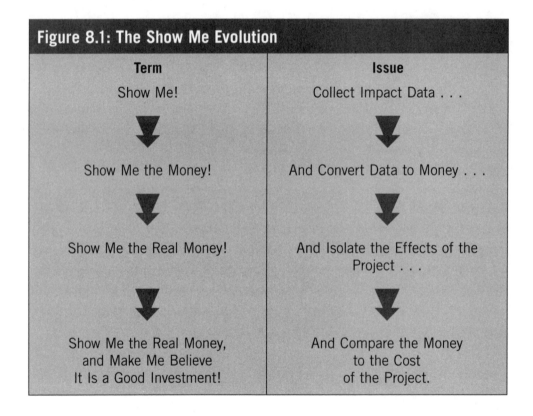

Figure 8.1: The Show Me Evolution

Term	Issue
Show Me!	Collect Impact Data . . .
Show Me the Money!	And Convert Data to Money . . .
Show Me the Real Money!	And Isolate the Effects of the Project . . .
Show Me the Real Money, and Make Me Believe It Is a Good Investment!	And Compare the Money to the Cost of the Project.

In short, ROI is a powerful objective that can serve as the answer to accountability concerns for some program sponsors and owners. For others, it conjures anxiety and disappointment.

BASIC ROI ISSUES

ROI objectives are based on formulas. Before presenting these formulas, we explore a few basic issues that must be understood before developing ROI objectives.

Definition

The term *return-on-investment* is occasionally—and sometimes intentionally—misused. This misuse broadly defines ROI, including any benefit from the program. For example, it is common to have someone claim, "This program has a great ROI." In that case, ROI is a vague concept. In this book, *return-on-investment* is precise and represents an actual value by comparing program costs to benefits. The two most common measures are the benefit-cost ratio (BCR) and the ROI percentage. Both are used, along with other approaches, to calculate the economic return or payback.

For many years, program leaders have sought to calculate the actual return-on-investment in programs and projects. If the program is considered an investment—not an expense—then it is appropriate to place it in the same funding process as other investments, such as the investment in equipment and facilities. Although the other investments might be different, executives and administrators often see them in the same light. Developing specific objectives that reflect the desired return on the investment is critical for the success of these programs.

Annualized Values: A Fundamental Concept

Using annualized values is an accepted practice for developing ROI in many organizations. All the formulas presented in this chapter use annualized values so that the first-year impact of the program can be calculated. This approach is a conservative way to develop ROI, as many short-term programs add value in the second or third year. For long-term programs, longer timeframes are used. For example, in an ROI analysis of a program involving self-directed teams in Litton Industries, a seven-year timeframe was used. For short-term programs that last only a few weeks, first-year values are more appropriate. Consequently, ROI objectives usually represent a year of monetary value measured not at the beginning of the program, but from the point where the impact is established.

HOW TO CONSTRUCT ROI OBJECTIVES

When selecting the approach to measure ROI and develop an objective, it is important to communicate to the target audience the formula used and the assumptions made in arriving at the decision to use this formula. This helps avoid confusion surrounding how the ROI value was actually developed. The two preferred methods, the benefit-cost ratio and the basic ROI formula, are described next.

Benefit-Cost Ratio

One of the oldest methods for evaluating projects and programs is cost-benefit analysis. This method compares the benefits of the program to the costs, resulting in a simple benefit-to-cost ratio. In formula form, the ratio is

$$BCR = \frac{Program\ Benefits}{Program\ Cost}$$

In simple terms, the BCR compares the annual economic benefits of the program to the costs. A BCR of 1 means that the benefits equal the costs. A BCR of 2, usually written as 2:1, indicates that for each dollar spent on the program, two dollars are returned in benefits. The following example illustrates the use of the BCR. A behavior modification program designed for managers and supervisors was implemented at an electric and gas utility. An ROI objective of 50 percent was established. This is the minimum acceptable ROI value, set by the client. This translates to a target BCR of 1.5:1. In a follow-up evaluation, action planning and business performance monitoring captured the benefits. The first-year payoff for the program was $477,750. The fully loaded implementation cost was $215,500. Thus, the ratio was:

$$BCR = \frac{\$477,750}{\$215,500} = 2.2:1$$

For every dollar invested in this program, 2.2 dollars in benefits were realized. The principal advantage of using this approach is that it avoids traditional financial measures, so confusion does not arise when comparing program investments with other investments in the company. Investment returns in plants, equipment, or subsidiaries, for example, are not usually reported using the benefit-cost ratio. Some program leaders prefer not to use the same formula to compare the return on program investments with the return on other investments. In these situations, the ROI for programs stands alone as a unique type of evaluation.

Unfortunately, no standards exist that constitute an acceptable BCR from the client perspective. A standard should be established within the organization, perhaps even for a specific type of program. However, a 1:1 ratio (break-even) is unacceptable for many programs. In others, a 1.25:1 ratio is required, where the benefits are 1.25 times the cost of the program.

ROI Formula

Perhaps the most appropriate formula for evaluating program investments is by comparing net program benefits to program costs. This is the traditional financial ROI and is directly related to the BCR. The comparison is expressed as a percentage when the fractional values are multiplied by 100. In formula form, the ROI is

$$\text{ROI (\%)} = \frac{\text{Net Program Benefits}}{\text{Program Costs}} \times 100$$

Net program benefits are program benefits minus costs. The ROI value is related to the BCR by a factor of 1. Subtract 1 from the BCR and multiply by 100 to get the ROI percentage. In the electric and gas utility example, a BCR of 2.2:1 is the same as an ROI value of 120 percent $(2.2 - 1 = 1.2$, and $1.2 \times 100 = 120$ percent). This value exceeds the 50 percent ROI objective. This formula is essentially the same as the ROI for capital investments. For example, when a firm builds a new plant, the ROI is developed by dividing annual earnings by the investment. The annual earnings are comparable to net benefits (annual benefits minus the cost). The investment is comparable to fully loaded program costs, which represent the investment in the program.

An ROI of 50 percent means that the costs are recovered, and an additional 50 percent of the costs are reported as "earnings." A program ROI of 150 percent indicates that the costs have been recovered, and an additional 1.5 times the costs are captured as "earnings."

The following example illustrates the ROI calculation. Public and private sector groups have been concerned about literacy and have developed a variety of programs to tackle the issue. Magnavox Electronics Systems Company was involved in a literacy program that focused on language and math skills for entry-level electrical and mechanical assemblers. The ROI objective was 25 percent. The results of the program were impressive. Productivity and quality alone yielded an annual value of $321,600. The fully loaded costs for the program were just $38,233. Thus, the return-on-investment was

$$\text{ROI (\%)} = \frac{\$321,600 - \$38,233}{\$38,233} \times 100 = 741\%$$

For each dollar invested, Magnavox received $7.41 in return after the costs of the literacy program had been recovered.

Using the ROI formula essentially places program investments on a level playing field with other investments using the same formula and similar concepts. The ROI calculation is easily understood by key management and financial executives who regularly use ROI with other investments.

ROI Interpretations

"Earnings" can be generated through increased sales or cost savings. In practice, more opportunities for cost savings occur than for profits. Cost savings can be generated when improvements in productivity, quality, efficiency, cycle time, or actual cost reduction occur. Of the nearly 500 studies we have reviewed, the vast majority were based on cost savings. Approximately 85 percent of the cases in the studies had a payoff based on output, quality, efficiency, time, or cost reduction. The others had a payoff based on sales increases, where the earnings were derived from the profit margin. This is important for nonprofits and public sector organizations for which the profit opportunity is often unavailable. Most programs will be connected directly to cost savings, or cost avoidance. ROI can still be developed in those settings, based on costs saved or avoided.

Financial executives have used the ROI approach for centuries. Still, this technique did not become widespread in industry for evaluating operating performance until the early 1920s. Conceptually, ROI has intrinsic appeal because it blends all the major ingredients of profitability into one number; the ROI statistic by itself can be compared with opportunities elsewhere (both inside and outside). Practically, however, ROI is an imperfect measurement that should be used in conjunction with other performance measurements (Horngren, 1982).

It is important that the formula outlined above be used in organizations. Deviations from or misuse of the formula can create confusion among users and finance and accounting staffs. The chief financial officer (CFO) and the finance and accounting staff should become partners in the use of ROI. Without their support, involvement, and commitment, using ROI on a wide-scale basis is difficult. Because of this relationship, the same financial terms must be used as those used and expected by the CFO.

Table 8.1 shows examples of misuse of financial terms in the literature. Terms such as *return-on-intelligence* (or *return-on-information*) abbreviated as ROI do nothing but confuse the CFO, who is thinking that ROI is the actual return-on-investment described above. Sometimes, *return-on-expectations* (ROE), *return-on-anticipation* (ROA), or *return-on-client expectation* (ROCE) are used, confusing the CFO, who is thinking *return-on-equity*, *return-on-assets*, and *return-on-capital employed*, respectively. Use of these terms in the calculation of payback of a program will do nothing but confuse others and perhaps cause you to lose the support of the finance and accounting staff. Other terms, such as *return-on-people*, *return-on-resources*, *return-on-technology*, and *return-on-objectives*, are often used, with almost no consistent financial calculations. The bottom line: Do not confuse the CFO. Consider this individual an ally, and use the same terminology, processes, and concepts when applying financial returns for programs.

Table 8.1: Misuse of Financial Terms

Term	Misuse	CFO Definition
ROI	Return-on-Information, Return-on-Intelligence, or Return-on-Inspiration	Return-on-Investment
ROE	Return-on-Expectation or Return-on-Effort	Return-on-Equity
ROA	Return-on-Anticipation	Return-on-Assets
ROCE	Return-on-Client Expectation	Return-on-Capital Employed
ROP	Return-on-People	??
ROR	Return-on-Resources	??
ROT	Return-on-Technology or Return-on-Training	??
ROW	Return-on-Web	??
ROO	Return-on-Objectives	??

Specific ROI Targets

Specific objectives for ROI should be developed before an evaluation study is undertaken. While no generally accepted standards exist, four strategies have been used to establish a minimum acceptable requirement, or hurdle rate, for ROI in a program. The first approach is to set the ROI using the same values used to invest in capital expenditures, such as equipment, facilities, and new companies. For North America, Western Europe, and most of the Asia Pacific area (including Australia and New Zealand), the cost of capital is quite low, and the internal hurdle rate for ROI is usually in the 15 to 20 percent range. Using this strategy, organizations would set the expected ROI at the same value expected from other investments.

A second strategy is to use an ROI minimum that represents a higher standard than the value required for other investments. This target value is above the percentage required for other types of investments. The rationale: The ROI process for programs is still relatively new and often involves subjective input, including estimations. Because of that, a higher standard is required or suggested. For most of North America, Western Europe, and the Asia Pacific area, this value is set at 25 percent.

A third strategy is to set the ROI value at a break-even point. A 0 percent ROI represents breakeven. This is equivalent to a BCR of 1. The rationale for this approach is an eagerness to recapture the cost of the program only. This is the ROI objective for many public sector organizations. If the funds expended for programs can be captured, value and benefit have come from the program through the intangible measures—which are not converted to monetary values—and the behavior change that is evident in the application and implementation data. Thus, some organizations will use a break-even point, under the philosophy that they are not attempting to make a profit from a particular program.

Finally, a fourth, and sometimes recommended, strategy is to let the client or program sponsor set the minimum acceptable ROI value. In this scenario, the individual who initiates, approves, sponsors, or supports the program establishes the acceptable ROI. Almost every program has a major sponsor, and that person may be willing to offer the acceptable value. This links the expectations of financial return directly to the expectations of the individual sponsoring the program.

OTHER ROI MEASURES

In addition to the traditional BCR and ROI formulas previously described, several other measures are occasionally used under the general term *return-on-*

investment. These measures are designed primarily for evaluating capital expenditures, but sometimes work their way into program or project evaluations.

Payback Period

The payback period is another common method for evaluating capital expenditures. With this approach, the annual cash proceeds (savings) produced by an investment are compared to the initial cash outlay required by the investment. Measurement is usually in terms of years and months. For example, if the cost savings generated from a program are constant each year, the payback period is determined by dividing the total original cash investment (development costs, expenses, and so forth) by the amount of the expected annual or actual savings (program benefits). To illustrate this calculation, assume that an initial program cost is $100,000 with a three-year useful life. The annual savings from the program is expected to be $40,000. Thus, the payback period becomes

$$\text{Payback Period} = \frac{\text{Total Investment}}{\text{Annual Savings}} = \frac{\$100,000}{\$40,000} = 2.5 \text{ Years}$$

The program will "pay back" the original investment in 2.5 years. The payback period is simple to use, but has the limitation of ignoring the time value of money. Thus, it has not enjoyed widespread use in evaluating program investments.

Discounted Cash Flow

Discounted cash flow is a method of evaluating investment opportunities in which certain values are assigned to the timing of the proceeds from the investment. The assumption, based on interest rates, is that a dollar earned today is more valuable than a dollar earned a year from now.

There are several ways to use the discounted cash flow concept to evaluate a program investment. The most common approach is the net present value of an investment. This approach compares the savings, year by year, with the outflow of cash required by the investment. The expected savings received each year is discounted by selected interest rates. The outflow of cash is also discounted by the same interest rate if the investment is ongoing, otherwise the initial outlay of cash is used. If the present value of the savings should exceed the present value of the outlays, after discounting at a common interest rate, management usually considers the investment to be acceptable. The discounted cash flow method has the advantage of ranking investments, but it becomes difficult to calculate.

Internal Rate of Return

The internal rate-of-return (IRR) method determines the interest rate required to make the present value of the cash flow equal to zero. It represents the maximum rate of interest that could be paid if all project funds were borrowed and the organization had to break even on the projects. The IRR considers the time value of money and is unaffected by the scale of the project. It can be used to rank alternatives or to make accept/reject decisions when a minimum rate of return is specified. A major weakness of the IRR method, however, is that it assumes all returns are reinvested at the same internal rate of return. This can make an investment alternative with a high rate of return look even better than it really is, and a project with a low rate of return look even worse. In practice, the IRR is rarely used to evaluate program investments.

CAUTIONS WHEN USING ROI

Because of the sensitivity around the use of ROI, caution is needed when developing, calculating, and communicating the return-on-investment. The use of ROI objectives and the implementation of the ROI process is a very important issue and a goal of many functions. The following cautions are offered when using ROI.

Take a Conservative Approach

Conservatism in ROI analysis builds accuracy and credibility. What matters most is how the target audience perceives the value of the data. A conservative approach is always recommended for both the numerator of the ROI formula (net program benefits) and the denominator (program costs.)

Use Caution

There are many ways to calculate the return on funds invested or assets employed. The ROI is just one of them. Although the calculation for ROI in your project uses the same basic formula as in capital investment evaluations, it might not be fully understood by the target group. Its calculation method and its meaning should be clearly communicated. More important, it should be an item accepted by management as an appropriate measure for program evaluation.

Involve Management

Management ultimately makes the decision as to whether an ROI value is acceptable. To the extent possible, management should be involved in setting the parameters for calculations and establishing targets by which programs are considered acceptable within the organization.

Fully Disclose the Assumptions and Methodology

When discussing the ROI Methodology and communicating data, it is important to fully disclose the process, steps, and assumptions used in the process.

Teach Others

Each time an ROI is calculated, the project leader should use this opportunity to educate other managers and colleagues in the organization. Even if it is not in their area of responsibility, these individuals will be able to see the value of this approach to evaluation. Also, when possible, each project should serve as a case study to educate the team on specific techniques and methods.

Not Everyone Will Buy Into ROI

Not every audience member will understand, appreciate, or accept the ROI calculation. For a variety of reasons, one or more individuals might not agree with the values. These individuals might be highly emotional about the concept of showing accountability for projects. Attempts to persuade them might be beyond the scope of the task at hand.

Do Not Boast About a High Return

It is not unusual to generate what appears to be a very high return-on-investment for a program. A project manager who boasts a high return will be open to potential criticism from others unless there are indisputable facts on which the calculation is grounded.

Choose the Time and Place for Debate

The time to debate the ROI Methodology is not during the project evaluation (unless it cannot be avoided). There are constructive venues for debate on the ROI process, such as in a special forum, among the project team, in an educational session, in professional literature, on panel discussions, or even during development of an ROI impact study. Debating at an inappropriate time or place can detract from the quality and quantity of information presented.

HOW TO USE ROI OBJECTIVES

Program Design

An ROI objective provides extreme focus. Not only must business impact measures improve, but they must improve enough to overcome the cost of the program. This sets a clear expectation—one that can create high levels of motivation or anxiety, depending on how individuals perceive the objectives. In planning, organizers create appreciation for the proper use of ROI. It might require education so participants understand their roles.

Program Facilitation

For facilitators, obviously, the pressure is on when an ROI is included. The focus is intense, and those involved must do what they can to make it work for them. For programs with potentially high impact, the ROI can be extremely motivational, as it places a significant challenge before the participants and facilitator.

Management and Executives

Perhaps the group that relates to ROI objectives most is the management team. Managers and executives involved in projects clearly see the project's value. Now they see that there is an ROI objective. Senior executives who approve the funding are much more satisfied with a project when there is an ROI objective. This enables them to rest comfortably, knowing that if the objective is met, the investment generates a positive return.

Marketing

There is no more powerful measure than a positive ROI to show the value of a project. When developed and calculated credibly, it can be used to convince others to become involved or persuade other sponsors to pursue similar projects. When the ROI is negative, stakeholders gain information as to what they could do to make it positive and successful. This is powerful data for all current and prospective stakeholders.

ROI Is Not for Every Program

ROI objectives should not be applied to every project or program. ROI objectives are appropriate for programs that meet criteria such as these:

> *Important to the organization to meet operating goals.* These programs are designed to add value. ROI may be helpful to show that value.
> *Closely linked to strategic initiatives.* Anything this important needs a high level of accountability.
> *Very expensive to implement.* An expensive program, requiring large amounts of resources, should be subjected to this level of accountability.
> *Highly visible and sometimes controversial.* These programs often require this level of accountability to satisfy the critics and the concerned.
> *Targeted at a large audience.* If a program is designed for all employees, it may be a candidate for ROI because of the exposure, resources, and time.
> *Of interest to top executives and administrators.* If top executives are interested in the ultimate impact of programs and projects, then the ROI should be developed.

These are only guidelines and should be considered within the context of the situation and the organization. Other criteria may also be appropriate. These criteria can be used in a process to sort out those programs most appropriate for this level of accountability.

It is also helpful to consider the programs for which ROI objectives are not appropriate. ROI is seldom appropriate for programs that are very short in duration, are very inexpensive, are legislated or required by regulation, are required by senior management, or serve as a basis to teach required skills for specific jobs. This is not meant to imply that an ROI objective (and subsequent ROI Methodology) cannot be implemented for these types of programs. However, when considering the limited resources for measurement and evaluation, careful use of these resources and time will result in evaluating more strategic types of programs.

FINAL THOUGHTS

This chapter explores the challenging yet rewarding issue of ROI objectives. Not every program should have an ROI objective. In fact, most programs should not. Expensive, high-profile, strategic programs are the most appropriate for an ROI objective. This chapter describes how the ROI objectives are developed using a variety of calculations, with the most common calculation being ROI expressed as a percentage. Use of an ROI objective should be pursued carefully and deliberately.

CHAPTER 9

Pulling It All Together

Although the previous chapters offer examples of how to develop objectives at the different levels, there is nothing like a case study to show how the process evolves. Chapter 1 presented three short case studies that described organization profile, the issues involved, and the objectives. However, the case studies did not show how the objectives were developed. The objectives were developed following important and necessary analyses and discussion, presented in chapter 2. The following case study shows how this is accomplished.

THE SITUATION

Global Financial Services (GFS) is a large international firm that offers a variety of financial services to clients. After analyzing its current sales practices and results, the firm identified the need to manage sales relationships more effectively. A task force comprising representatives from field sales, marketing, financial consulting, information technology, and education and training examined several solutions for improving relationships, including customer-contact software packages. The firm chose to implement a software package designed to turn contacts into relationships and relationships into increased sales. The software features a flexible customer database, easy contact entry, a calendar, and a to-do list. It enables quick and effective customer communication and is designed for use with customized reports.

This project represented a tremendous amount of money—approximately $1 million total for the proposed software purchase, training, networking for the software, and time away from work. This million-dollar decision prompted a detailed analysis in which objectives were needed at all levels.

The project director met with a variety of stakeholders to secure input for the objectives. Those involved in the meeting included the analyst who conducted the initial needs assessment, a marketing manager who understands the marketing dynamics, the project requestor (sponsor), a sales representative from the software supplier, a district sales manager who manages the relationship managers (RMs), two RMs (sales representatives), the facilitator for the program, and the project evaluator.

INPUT OBJECTIVES

The software implementation and training had to be developed quickly and provided to all 4,000 RMs so the benefits of the project could be realized. A pilot program was envisioned that could be implemented with a small number of RMs (120) and the results used quickly to see if there was a positive ROI before pursuing the complete purchase and networking of the system. GFS has RMs in 20 regional offices, and it was preferred that the training be conducted in those offices to minimize hotel and travel costs and disruption. Regional training centers were used in each of the regional offices. It was critical for the budget not to exceed the anticipated $700,000 in direct costs associated with the software, networking, and training delivery. After the pilot was approved and the training complete, the project was to be implemented within one month. The pilot program can be evaluated in three months.

Questions for Discussion

1. What input topics should be addressed?

    _____

    _____

    _____

    _____

    _____

2. Write the specific input objectives that represent the most critical areas.

    _____

    _____

    _____

    _____

    _____

Responses to Discussion Questions

1. These topics should perhaps be addressed:
   a. *Delivery.* Focus on a pilot program first.
   b. *Timing.* To ensure that the dates are met.
   c. *Budgets.* Stay within budget.
   d. *Audience.* Define the proper audience. (Does this involve support staff?)
   e. *Duration.* Only one day.
   f. *Location.* Conduct it in the regional offices.
   g. *Disruption.* Minimize the disruption of taking the relationship managers away from normal customer work.

2. The project will be delivered with these specific objectives:
   a. Upon completion, direct costs will be less than $700,000.
   b. Conduct a pilot program with 120 participants, with evaluation completed within three months.
   c. Full implementation should be completed within one month after the pilot evaluation is complete.
   d. The program will involve relationship sales managers only with no support staff.
   e. The one-day workshop will be conducted at regional training offices with no travel involved.
   f. A repeat session will be conducted—all to be completed within one month.

REACTION OBJECTIVES

Next, the discussion focused on how participants should react to the workshop, the software, and their use of the software. The group concluded that the workshop should be important to participants and their work. The principal concern was whether they would actually use the software. GFS has a history of buying software for the sales team, and then the product goes unused for a variety of reasons, primarily because the sales staff did not see the benefit. Also, the sales team members must see this software as an aid to their success. "What's in it for me?" is a huge issue. "If I am going to take my time away from my customers, this better be worth it," is the prevailing attitude. They need to see the software as useful and helpful in driving sales and improving customer satisfaction.

Questions for Discussion

1. What areas would you consider measuring at the reaction level?

   _____

   _____

   _____

   _____

   _____

   _____

2. Construct the reaction objectives that represent the most important areas.

   _____

   _____

   _____

   _____

   _____

   _____

Responses to Discussion Questions

1. The key areas would be as follows:
   a. *What is in it for me?* They must see that this will increase sales.
   b. *Relevance to my work.* It must tackle the problem directly or improve the current job situation.
   c. *Useful to me personally.* This must be user friendly and not complicated.
   d. *Intent to use.* They must indicate an intent to use, perhaps even with planned action. Without this, it might fail.
   e. *Recommend to others.* Since all relationship sales managers must attend, it would help the situation if the early participants would recommend this to later participants.

2. At the end of this one-day workshop, the participant should rate the following measures 4 or more on a 5-point scale:
   a. The software is important to my current success.
   b. It is relevant to my work and clients.
   c. It is easy to use.
   d. I intend to use the software.
   e. I will recommend that others attend this.

LEARNING OBJECTIVES

After some discussion with the software supplier and the RMs, the key information that the RMs must know began to emerge. The team concluded that there was a variety of features and benefits that they must know and that perhaps a checklist or a quiz would be appropriate. These items were straightforward features and routines that could be learned easily. Participants must also use the software in the classroom and demonstrate certain features. Specifically, the planning group wanted them to demonstrate that they know how to

> - enter a new contact
> - create a mail-merge document
> - create a query
> - send a customized response
> - create a call report
> - create a sales data summary
> - create a status report.

The facilitator should observe each participant to ensure that he or she can correctly perform the tasks.

Questions for Discussion

1. What areas should be covered in the learning objectives?

   _____

   _____

   _____

   _____

   _____

   _____

2. Write the specific learning objectives.

   _____

   _____

   _____

   _____

   _____

Responses to Discussion Questions

1. The objectives should cover basic knowledge and skills related to the software, including knowledge of the features and benefits of the system and the ability to demonstrate this knowledge.
2. After completing this workshop
   a. participants will score 75 or better on a test measuring the features and benefits of the new software (80 percent target)
   b. given the complete software package, participants will demonstrate to the facilitator five of the following seven features within 12 minutes with zero errors:

   > enter a new contact
   > create a mail-merge document
   > create a query
   > send a customized response
   > create a call report
   > create a data summary
   > create a status report.

APPLICATION OBJECTIVES

Next, the group focused on application objectives. The concern centered on the expectations of the relationship managers: "What do we want them to do, and when do we want them to do it?" This becomes critical, as this audience has a history of ignoring new tools and software. Detailed objectives were needed not only to check the progress, but to create expectation and drive the desired performance. The first issue involved the immediate use of the new system for customer-contact management. It is critical for users to enter new clients and new prospects directly into the system as they are developed. It is equally important to begin merging the current contacts into this new system.

In terms of usage, there are many features that RMs should be using routinely. Fortunately, the software had built-in, user-performance profiles that track how often they use the software, what they are using, how accurately they are using it, and if major parts of the process are omitted. This user-performance profile has a scoring mechanism to indicate how well RMs are using the software. One hundred percent is perfect use. After some discussion, the team decided that to achieve an 80 percent score in four weeks would be acceptable. Also, they wanted this software to generate additional follow-ups. While the follow-ups provide a consequence (such as sales or customer satisfaction), it is important for the relationship managers to use the system to schedule more follow-ups. Consequently, the number of calls and appointments should increase. This is the culmination of the use of the system.

Questions for Discussion

1. Specifically what areas should be explored in the application objectives?

_____

_____

_____

_____

_____

_____

2. Write the specific application objectives.

_____

_____

_____

_____

_____

_____

Responses to Discussion Questions

1. The areas that should be explored in the application objectives are these:

   a. *User-performance profile.* A host of functions and activities and use of the software is tracked automatically.

   b. *Entering names in the database.* New contacts, new prospects, and new customers.

   c. *Merging existing documents in the system.* Bringing all of the current contacts and customers into the system.

   d. *Planning follow-ups.* This is the actual scheduling of follow-ups with an individual. There is sometimes confusion about whether this should be Level 3 or Level 4. Essentially, the RMs are scheduling more follow-ups than normal. Therefore, this is something that they are doing (that is, increasing performance) as a result of the software. The consequences of the follow-up will occur later as sales are generated or customer satisfaction is increased.

   e. *Barriers and enablers.* These are always tracked to understand clearly what got in the way and what has helped with software usage.

2. After the workshop is completed, participants will

   a. enter new contacts, new prospects, and new customers within one day of obtaining the information

   b. merge the current customer database into the new system within one week

   c. use the software routinely as reflected in an 80 percent user performance profile score out of a possible 100 percent, which will occur three weeks after the workshop

   d. increase the number of weekly planned follow-ups with customers by 10 percent within three weeks

   e. in one month, identify the barriers that have prevented them from using this system successfully

   f. in one month, identify the enablers that have helped them use this system to the extent that they have.

IMPACT OBJECTIVES

The discussion among the planning team members moved to impact objectives—a much easier step for the group. These measures framed the rationale for implementing the program in the first place. However, several issues needed further discussion. While the program was perceived as a tool to drive sales with existing customers, improve customer satisfaction, and reduce complaints, additional discussion centered on the cause-and-effect relationship. In other words, "Is this software actually going to do what we want it to do?" Although this was the premise of the initial needs assessment, it was helpful to have the dialogue about how to know it would make the difference.

Some initial analysis revealed that customers were complaining about response time on the part of the RMs. A deeper analysis revealed that some customers were not recommending the firm to others. In a few cases, they were going to a competitor. The issue seemed to center on managing communication with the customer in a timely and productive manner. This software is intended to do just that—ensure that communication is smooth and timely and keeps RMs focused on service.

Consequently, this software should certainly reduce response time, although there is no formal way to measure it in the system. That is, when a customer calls or has an inquiry, nothing in the system measures the time taken to respond to that particular customer. Even this software does not do that. While it is not measured, it is certainly an issue that can be monitored on a perception basis. Also, customer satisfaction should be connected to the software use, along with increasing revenue with current customers and reducing customer complaints. The logic: If RMs respond quickly and reduce complaints, customer satisfaction increases and sales increase.

Questions for Discussion

1. What issues should the impact objectives address?

_____

_____

_____

_____

_____

_____

2. Write the impact objectives.

_____

_____

_____

_____

_____

_____

Responses to Discussion Questions

1. The following areas are considered important for the impact objectives:

   a. *Reduce response time.* Although this is not measured, it is an important consequence measure. Improvement can be captured on a perception basis.

   b. *Reduce customer complaints.* Particularly those that are based on delays in acquiring information.

   c. *Customer satisfaction.* Measured in a customer satisfaction composite survey index.

   d. *Sales with existing customers.* Under the rationale that if RMs kept closer correspondence, commitment, and communication, then it would be easier for customers to remain with the firm and provide more opportunity to increase the level of business.

2. Within three months of implementation, there should be

   a. a reduction in the time to respond to customer inquiries and requests

   b. a reduction in the number of customer complaints regarding missed deadlines, late responses, and failure to complete transactions

   c. an increase in the customer satisfaction composite survey index by 20 percent at the next survey (in six months)

   d. an increase in sales for existing customers.

ROI OBJECTIVES

The final objective is the ROI objective. It had been decided earlier that the program would be evaluated at ROI on a pilot basis to see if it should be implemented throughout the company. A positive ROI was needed, because it would clearly reflect that this expense is an investment and that there is a positive return on that investment. Determining the precise amount stirred up some debate. Some members of the team thought that it should be held to the same standard as when they buy another company. At GFS, the ROI hurdle rate is 17 percent for major capital expenditures. Some suggested that a standard should be set higher than the company's hurdle rate—maybe 20 percent. Others thought it would be best to let the sponsor select the number, because a small sample is being used to make a decision about the entire company. Still others indicated that a breakeven on this project—which would be 0 percent ROI—would be okay. This argument was based on the fact that there are some intangibles that will not be converted to money, such as customer satisfaction. Also, more than likely, the customer response time is going to be an intangible, because they had no way of easily and credibly converting it to money.

Questions for Discussion

1. What do you recommend for an ROI objective and why?

_____

_____

_____

_____

_____

_____

2. How should it be worded?

_____

_____

_____

_____

_____

_____

Responses to Discussion Questions

1. The group chose ROI and the benefit-cost ratio as two measures. The client asked for 25 percent return. This seemed to be a rational value and was only slightly above the hurdle rate for other capital projects.

2. The actual wording: "After three months, and based on one year of value, the project should attain a benefit-cost ratio of 1.25:1 and represent an ROI value of 25 percent, using a first year of benefits."

References

Bloom, B.S. (Ed.). *Taxonomy of Educational Objectives*. New York: David McKay Company Inc., 1956.

Dixon, M.N. *Evaluation, a Tool for Improving HRD Quality*. San Francisco: Pfeiffer, 1990.

Gupta, K. A *Practical Guide to Needs Assessment*. San Francisco: Jossey-Bass, 1999.

Horngren, C.T. *Cost Accounting*, 5th ed. Englewood Cliffs, New Jersey: Prentice-Hall, 1982.

Kaplan, R.S., & Norton, D.P. *The Balanced Scorecard: Translating Strategy Into Action*. Boston: Harvard Business School Press, 1996.

Langdon, D., Whiteside, K., & McKenna, M. (Eds.). *Intervention Resource Guide: 50 Performance Improvement Tools*. San Francisco: Pfeiffer, 1999.

Mager, R.F. *Preparing Instructional Objectives*, rev. 2d ed. Belmont, California: Lake Publishing Company, 1984.

Mager, R.F. *Preparing Instructional Objectives: A Critical Tool in the Development of Effective Instruction*, 3d ed. Atlanta: CEP Press, 1997.

Phillips, J.J., & Phillips, P.P. *Measuring ROI in the Public Sector*. Alexandria, Virginia: ASTD Press, 2002.

Phillips, J.J., & Phillips, P.P. *ROI at Work: Best-Practice Case Studies from the Real World*. Alexandria, Virginia: ASTD Press, 2005.

Phillips, J.J., & Phillips, P.P. *Show Me the Money: How to Determine ROI in People, Projects, and Programs*. San Francisco: Berrett-Koehler Publishers Inc., 2007.

Phillips, J.J., & Zuniga, L. *Costs and ROI: Evaluating at the Ultimate Level.* San Francisco: Pfeiffer, 2008.

Phillips, J.J., Myhill M., & McDonough, J. *Proving the Value of Meetings and Events.* Birmingham, Alabama: ROI Institute and MPI, 2007.

Phillips, J.J., Phillips, P.P., Stone, R.D., & Burkett, H. *The ROI Fieldbook: Strategies for Implementing ROI in HR and Training.* Burlington, Massachusetts: Butterworth-Heinemann, 2007.

Phillips, P.P., & Phillips, J.J. *Proving the Value of HR: ROI Case Studies.* Birmingham, Alabama: ROI Institute and MPI, 2007.

Schrock, S., & Coscarelli, W. *Criterion-Referenced Test Development*, 2d ed. Silver Spring, Maryland: ISPI, 2000.

Responses to Exercises

Chapter 3—What's Wrong With These Input Objectives?

1. For this objective, more definition is needed. A specific date or perhaps incremental deadlines should be set.

2. This objective is nonspecific and contains two items that should be separated and defined with more detail. *Inexpensive* is an imprecise term; a budget amount should be given. *Latest technology* should be defined, at least to the extent that someone reading the objective can identify the specific type of technology and make a smart financial decision.

3. This is more a reaction objective than an input objective. It defines the desired stakeholders' reaction, not necessarily what goes into the project. It also is imprecise.

4. *Employees* needs further definition. Does it refer to frontline sales representatives? If so, is it restricted to those with direct contact with sales? What about sales support and marketing? What about customer-complaint and call centers? Specific details are needed.

5. This needs more definition, such as the number of hours and even the amount of disruption over time.

Chapter 4—What's Wrong With These Reaction Objectives?

1. The word *like* has many interpretations. *Like* should be better defined.

2. *Understood* is vague and not necessarily a reaction objective. It fits better in the learning category.

3. Again, more precise wording is needed. *Overall satisfaction* is an often-used phrase, but provides little understanding of project or program success. If participants are not satisfied, it's difficult to understand why unless other objectives are included. It might be important for some organizations to recognize participants' overall satisfaction, but by no means should this be the only measure.

4. The word *stimulating* is vague. However, if the word *stimulating* is to be used, the scale should read from "not very stimulating" to "very stimulating."

5. The wording is awkward, and the range of difficulty is not defined. The objective could be scores ranging from 3 to 4, for example. A scale, perhaps from 1 to 5, with 5 being "very difficult," should be noted.

Chapter 5—What's Wrong With These Learning Objectives?

1. This objective has several problems. First, the one-hour module is not a condition. It describes a procedure, not the conditions under which the performance will occur. No specific performance is stated. The statement needs an action verb.

2. The statement has little meaning, except that participants will learn something. The result of the learning is unclear—no performance is identified.

3. This is a goal and not necessarily an objective. *Understanding* is a vague word, and *leadership* is a broad subject.

4. Although it involves an important issue, the meaning of this objective is unclear and not performance based.

5. The objective is vague and not performance based. Also, two different issues are addressed.

6. *Demonstrate* is a trap word that often leads us to believe it is saying something specific when it is not. This objective needs more specifics about how knowledge will be demonstrated.

7. This objective is not performance based. Underlining a word does not necessarily add emphasis. More specifics are needed.

8. While this is an important statement, it is not an objective because it lacks specifics and a basis for performance.

Chapter 6—What's Wrong With These Application Objectives?

1. This is not specific. The topic is too broad. It would be difficult to have any accurate assessment with this objective.
2. This objective is actually a Level 2 (Learning) objective and not a very good one at that. The word *understanding* is weak.
3. This is still a Level 2 objective, as the participants are demonstrating what they know or what they know how to do. It is not an on-the-job application. A simulation is replicating a task, process, or procedure. It's not the real thing.
4. This is not very specific. The phrase *much better* does not help the situation. More detail about communication is needed.
5. This is a Level 1 (Reaction) objective, although it occurs two months after the program.
6. This is a vague objective. It does not detail what the supervisor is doing that employees perceive to be effective, a potential consequence of supervisory behavior.
7. This is still a Level 2 (Learning) objective, although the customer is live. The participant is being observed, so the performance might not mirror what would happen in an unobserved scenario. Actual job behavior is needed at Level 3.
8. While this is a Level 3 objective, it lacks specificity. What type of meetings? How will necessity of a meeting be defined? What timeframe is attached to this objective?

Chapter 7—What's Wrong With These Impact Objectives?

1. This lacks specificity in terms of the amount of the increase and the time in which it should occur. The amount of increase could be left vague if individual objectives are set for all those involved in the project.
2. This is vague and perhaps misleading. What exactly is the leadership profile? If it is leadership behavior, it is more appropriately a Level 3 objective and may be measured by a feedback instrument, such as a 360-degree feedback process. If it is the perceived effectiveness of the leadership team, then it alludes to a Level 4 objective, but it is too vague to measure. Specificity is needed.

3. This is a misleading objective. If capability is defined as the knowledge and skills of employees, then this is a Level 2 (Learning) measure. All the learning that has occurred in the project collectively increases the capability of the organization. If the objective reflects what the employee does with the capability, then the objective represents Level 3 (Application). If the intent is to measure the consequences of that application, then the objective should reflect this intended impact—Level 4 (Impact).

4. Two objectives are combined. Neither objective is clear. Specificity is lacking in terms of the amount of decrease and the time in which the improvement should occur.

5. This is more than likely a Level 3 objective. More definition is needed for *user performance profile*. If the profile suggests how individuals are performing, it becomes a Level 3 measure. If it also includes consequences, such as error rates and productivity, then it is Level 4, as well. It is best to separate the objectives. Again, they need to be specific.

6. This objective is Level 3 (Application). The word *implementation* usually means the process is being used, people are involved and are working on projects, actions are on schedule, teams are being trained, and so forth. Also, implementation should reflect a time requirement. If implementation also means having success with a cost savings in green-belt and black-belt projects, then it is an impact objective. The key is to define the implementation measure.

7. Again, this is vague. *Effectiveness* should be defined. Most definitions would focus effectiveness on Level 3—employees are performing in a particular way. However, if effectiveness is defined as the impact employees are having in their work units, then it would be pushed to Level 4. The key is definition.

8. The meaning of *efficiency* needs clarification, as it has many different definitions. Is it time based, such as how quickly things are being done? Is it per-person based, such as how much is accomplished per employee? Or is it merely the cost of something? Definitions are critical.

9. This is a Level 1 (Reaction) objective, not a consequence. There could be a fine line of interpretation. A consequence of the project would be, "As a result of this project, the workforce perceives the technology function as highly valuable." The consequence is that employees have changed their perception of the function. Merely measuring the perception of a project in terms of its success is measuring a reaction.

Matching Objectives
with Evaluation

Instructions

Take this simple test to check your knowledge about the different levels of objectives. Indicate the level of evaluation corresponding to each objective in the list. Each objective begins with the statement, "After completing this program or project, participants should do the following." So, have a go, and see how well you know the levels. We'll review responses afterward. Use the corresponding numbers below for your answers:

1. Reaction
2. Learning
3. Application
4. Impact
5. Return-on-Investment

Table B.1: Quiz: Identify the Level of Objective

Objective	Level
After completing this program or project, participants should:	
1. Improve work group productivity by 20 percent in six months.	_____
2. Initiate at least three cost-reduction projects in 15 days.	_____
3. Achieve an average cost reduction of $20,000 per project in six months.	_____
4. Increase the use of counseling skills in 90 percent of situations where work habits are unacceptable.	_____
5. Achieve a 2:1 benefit-cost ratio (BCR) one year after the new gain-sharing program is implemented.	_____
6. Identify the five critical steps an employee must take to access and use the employee assistance plan.	_____
7. Increase the external customer satisfaction index by 25 percent in three months.	_____
8. Address customer complaints with a five-step process in 95 percent of complaint situations.	_____
9. Not have an adverse reaction to the absenteeism policy within 90 days of implementation.	_____
10. Achieve a leadership-simulation score average of 75 out of a possible 100 in three weeks.	_____
11. Conduct a performance review meeting with direct reports within two weeks to establish performance improvement goals.	_____
12. Provide a 4 out of 5 rating on the appropriateness of a new ethics policy.	_____
13. Decrease the time to recruit engineers from 35 days to 20 days in six months.	_____

14. Complete all the steps on the action plans in three months.	———————
15. Perceive the flextime schedule to be useful (70 percent "yes").	———————
16. Be involved in a career enhancement program at a rate of 15 percent of nonmanagerial staff.	———————
17. Decrease the amount of time to complete a project.	———————
18. Achieve a post-test score increase of 30 percent over pre-test.	———————
19. Use new software daily as reflected in an 80 percent score of an unscheduled audit of use in three weeks.	———————
20. Submit ideas or suggestions for improvement in the first year (10 percent target).	———————

Responses to Quiz

1. Improve work group productivity by 20 percent in six months (4). This is an impact objective, clearly showing the consequences of doing something different in the work unit. That different approach, process, or application of new skills or knowledge has improved productivity.

2. Initiate at least three cost-reduction projects in 15 days (3). This objective represents action. Participants have initiated projects, but have not completed them. The projects will take several months to complete, and the fact that they are not yet complete means this is not an impact objective.

3. Achieve an average cost reduction of $20,000 per project in six months (4). This is an impact objective and is connected to the previous objective. It is the consequence of completing the project. The previous objective focused on getting participants to take action, while this one speaks to the consequences of that action.

4. Increase the use of counseling skills in 90 percent of situations where work habits are unacceptable (3). This use of skills represents application. Participants are applying what was learned in a basic supervisory skill-building program.

5. Achieve a 2:1 benefit-cost ratio (BCR) one year after the new gain-sharing program is implemented (5). This is ROI. The BCR is one way to show benefits versus costs. Incidentally, a 2:1 BCR is a 100 percent ROI, as detailed in chapter 8.

6. Identify the five critical steps an employee must take to access and use the employee assistance plan (2). This learning objective indicates what employees must learn or know to make the plan work for them.

7. Increase the external customer satisfaction index by 25 percent in three months (4). This is an impact objective—a consequence of doing something different with customers that results in a higher degree of satisfaction.

8. Address customer complaints with a five-step process in 95 percent of complaint situations (3). This application objective indicates use of a particular process. The objective involves a criterion as well.

9. Not have an adverse reaction to the absenteeism policy within 90 days of implementation (1). In this case, it's important for the reaction to be at least neutral, if not positive. The key is to avoid a negative reaction when changing current policies or practices. Employees might perceive a loss of control or a loss of freedom they previously had. The focus of this reaction objective is keeping attitudes in check.

10. Achieve a leadership-simulation score average of 75 out of a possible 100 in three weeks (2). This is a learning objective. Simulation replicates a process, task, or procedure and measures the extent to which participants know how to do something. Consequently, a simulation score measures knowledge or skills gained.

11. Conduct a performance review meeting with direct reports within two weeks to establish performance improvement goals (3). This application objective is part of a performance management system introduced through a formal session where supervisors and managers learned how to set performance improvement goals. These supervisors were required to conduct the review meeting with direct reports, with action items and goals posted online in the performance management system.

12. Provide a 4 out of 5 rating on the appropriateness of a new ethics policy (1). This objective focuses on reaction to the policy. The concern is that employees should perceive that the actions taken to address ethics are appropriate.

13. Decrease the time to recruit engineers from 35 days to 20 days in six months (4). This is an impact objective, a consequence of changing the recruiting process. Essentially, we are trying something different (Level 3) and, consequently, the recruiting time decreases.

14. Complete all the steps on the action plans in three months (3). This is an application objective, as the steps must be completed. Sometimes action plans do contain impact consequences and can actually be involved at both Level 3 and 4 objectives; but, not knowing that, the most appropriate response would be 3, application.

15. Perceive the flextime schedule to be useful (70 percent "yes") (1). This is a reaction objective, as individuals react to the new flex system. When these types of systems are implemented, it is important for participants to perceive the systems as useful to them personally.

16. Be involved in a career enhancement program at a rate of 15 percent of nonmanagerial staff (3). This is a voluntary career enhancement program where participants have a choice to be involved. If they want to be involved, they must complete an assessment, plan a career development program, and work on the process until it is completed.

17. Decrease the amount of time to complete a project (4). This impact objective reflects a consequence of applying a different process in the project management scenario. It could involve implementing software, conducting project management training, or establishing a project management office. One of the consequences of the new process after it is implemented and applied (Level 3) is that project management time decreases (Level 4).

18. Achieve a post-test score increase of 30 percent over pre-test (2). This is a bit tricky, but normally it would represent a learning objective. Pre- and post-testing usually measure learning; however, pre/post data can be developed at Levels 1, 2, 3, or 4. At Level 3, for instance, we could have pre/post measures on changes in skills. For example, a classic way to measure leadership development skills is a 360-degree feedback process, where behavioral data are taken from a variety of sources and integrated for a composite rating. This process could be conducted prior to a leadership development program as a pre-assessment and conducted three months after the program for a post-assessment. The pre/post difference shows a change in behavior; hence, it reflects application.

19. Use new software daily as reflected in an 80 percent score of an unscheduled audit of use in three weeks (3). This objective is an application objective dealing with actual use of the software. In this situation, an appointed person will come to the workplace and audit the use of the software by examining routine work and developing user profiles. This is an assessment of application of the software.

20. Submit ideas or suggestions for improvement in the first year (10 percent target) (3). During the launch of this employee suggestion pro-

gram, employees are introduced to the program (measure reaction), they learn how to submit suggestions (measure learning), and then they submit suggestions (application). If the suggestion is accepted, any cost savings are realized, and an impact is realized. The goal is to have 10 percent of employees submit suggestions.

We hope you find that you have mastered the ability to create objectives. They are powerful and necessary and ensure programs and projects are positioned to achieve results!

Beyond Learning Objectives: Develop Measurable Objectives That Link to the Bottom Line

An Interactive Workshop from the ROI Institute

Description

One of the best ways to transform your present approach to developing more powerful, specific, and results-based objectives is to participate in a one-day workshop offered by the ROI Institute. This workshop, conducted by the authors of this book or other senior members of the ROI Institute, will focus on the hands-on application with practice sessions to learn how to develop all levels of objectives. The specific topics covered are

> - the importance of objectives—how they make a difference
> - the origin of objectives—who, what, when, where, and how
> - developing input objectives
> - developing reaction objectives
> - developing learning objectives

> developing application objectives
> developing impact objectives
> developing ROI objectives
> making it work routinely—getting into the habit
> next steps.

Workshop Objectives

After being involved in the workshop, participations should

> perceive the workshop as valuable to their current work
> view the workshop as important to their projects
> see the material as practical in use.

After completing the workshop, participants should be able to

> describe the importance of objectives to various stakeholder groups, including clients
> uncover the precise objectives from those individuals who understand the project most
> construct objectives at each of the levels given a detailed description and documentation of the project.

After completing the workshop and returning to the workplace, participants should

> develop input, reaction, learning, and application objectives for at least 70 percent of new projects and programs
> develop impact objectives for at least 30 percent of new projects and programs
> develop ROI objectives for at least 10 percent of new projects and programs
> use the objectives to drive results from the project.

After completing the workshop and at the end of six months

> programs and projects will achieve increased results
> participants will be motivated to drive results
> the relationships with various stakeholders will improve.

The materials for the workshop includes a 50-page workbook containing tips, techniques, exercises, case studies, and practice opportunities; a copy of this book *Beyond Learning Objectives: Develop Measurable Objectives That Link to the Bottom Line*, and an additional case study.

About the Authors

Jack J. Phillips, PhD

Dr. Jack J. Phillips is a world-renowned expert on accountability, measurement, and evaluation. Phillips provides consulting services for *Fortune* 500 companies and major global organizations. The author or editor of more than 50 books, he conducts workshops and presents at conferences throughout the world.

Phillips has received several awards for his books and work. On two occasions, *Meeting News* named him one of the 25 Most Influential People in the Meetings and Events Industry, based on his work on ROI. The Society for Human Resource Management presented him an award for one of his books and honored a Phillips ROI study with its highest award for creativity. The American Society for Training & Development gave him its highest award, Distinguished Contribution to Workplace Learning and Development, for his work on ROI.

His expertise in measurement and evaluation is based on more than 27 years of corporate experience in the aerospace, textile, metals, construction materials, and banking industries. Phillips has served as training and development manager at two *Fortune* 500 firms, as senior human resource officer at two firms, as president of a regional bank, and as management professor at a major state university.

This background led Phillips to develop the ROI Methodology—a revolutionary process that provides bottom-line figures and accountability for all types of learning, performance improvement, human resource, technology, and public policy programs.

Phillips regularly consults with clients in manufacturing, service, and government organizations in 44 countries in North and South America, Europe, Africa, Australia, and Asia.

Books most recently authored by Phillips include *Return on Investment in Meetings and Events: Tools and Techniques to Measure the Success of All Types of Meetings and Events* (Elsevier, 2008); *ROI for Technology Projects: Measuring and Delivering Value* (Elsevier, 2007); *Show Me the Money: How to Determine ROI in People, Projects, and Programs* (Berrett-Koehler, 2007); *The Value of Learning* (Pfeiffer, 2007); *How to Build a Successful Consulting Practice* (McGraw-Hill, 2006); *Investing in Your Company's Human Capital: Strategies to Avoid Spending Too Much or Too Little* (Amacom, 2005); *Proving the Value of HR: How and Why to Measure ROI* (SHRM, 2005); *The Leadership Scorecard* (Elsevier Butterworth-Heinemann, 2004); *Managing Employee Retention* (Elsevier Butterworth-Heinemann, 2003); *Return on Investment in Training and Performance Improvement Programs*, 2nd ed. (Elsevier Butterworth-Heinemann, 2003); *The Project Management Scorecard* (Elsevier Butterworth-Heinemann, 2002); *How to Measure Training Results* (McGraw-Hill, 2002); *The Human Resources Scorecard: Measuring the Return on Investment* (Elsevier Butterworth-Heinemann, 2001); *The Consultant's Scorecard* (McGraw-Hill, 2000); and *Performance Analysis and Consulting* (ASTD Press, 2000). Phillips served as series editor for ASTD's In Action casebook series, an ambitious publishing project featuring 30 titles. He currently serves as series editor for Elsevier Butterworth-Heinemann's Improving Human Performance series and for Pfeiffer's new series on Measurement and Evaluation.

Phillips has undergraduate degrees in electrical engineering, physics, and mathematics; a master's degree in Decision Sciences from Georgia State University; and a PhD in Human Resource Management from the University of Alabama. He has served on the boards of several private businesses—including two NASDAQ companies—and several nonprofits and associations, including ASTD. He is chairman of the ROI Institute Inc. and can be reached at 205.678.8101 or by email at jack@roiinstitute.net.

Patricia P. Phillips, PhD

Dr. Patricia P. Phillips is president and CEO of the ROI Institute Inc., the leading source of ROI competency building, implementation support, networking, and research. A renowned expert in measurement and evaluation, she helps organizations implement the ROI Methodology in countries around the world, including South Africa, Australia, Chile, Brazil, Romania, Ireland, Canada, and the United States.

Since 1997, following a 13-year career in the electric utility industry, Phillips has embraced the ROI Methodology by committing herself to ongoing research and practice. To this end, Phillips has implemented ROI in private sector and public sector organizations. She has conducted ROI impact studies on programs such as leadership development, sales, new-hire orientation, human performance improvement, K-12 educator development, and educators' National Board Certification mentoring. Her current work includes research and application of the ROI Methodology in workforce development, community development, and social sector programs.

As facilitator of the ROI Certification process and ASTD's ROI and Measuring and Evaluating Learning Workshops and as adjunct professor for graduate-level evaluation courses, Phillips teaches others to implement the ROI Methodology. She serves on numerous doctoral dissertation committees, assisting students as they develop their own research on measurement, evaluation, and ROI.

Phillips speaks on the topic of ROI at conferences such as ASTD's International Conference and Exposition, ISPI's International Conference, KnowledgeAdvisors Metrics Symposium, *Training Magazine*'s annual conference, and the ROI Global Conference held in countries around the world. She is often heard over the Internet as she presents the ROI Methodology to a wide variety of audiences via webcast.

Phillips's academic accomplishments include a PhD in International Development and a master's degree in Public and Private Management. She is certified in ROI evaluation and has been awarded the designations of Certified Professional in Learning and Performance and Certified Performance Technologist. She contributes to a variety of journals and has authored a number of books on the subject of accountability and ROI, including *Return on Investment in Meetings and Events: Tools and Techniques to Measure the Success of All Types of Meetings and Events* (Elsevier, 2008); *Show Me the Money: How to Determine ROI in People, Projects, and Programs* (Berrett-Koehler, 2007); *The Value of Learning* (Pfeiffer, 2007); *Return on Investment*

Basics (ASTD Press, 2005); *Proving the Value of HR: How and Why to Measure ROI* (SHRM, 2005); *ROI at Work* (ASTD Press, 2005); *Make Training Evaluation Work* (ASTD Press, 2004); *The Bottom Line on ROI* (Center for Effective Performance, 2002), which won the 2003 ISPI Award of Excellence; the ASTD In Action casebooks *Measuring ROI in the Public Sector* (2002), *Retaining Your Best Employees* (2002), and *Measuring Return on Investment* Vol. III (2001); the ASTD *Infoline* series, including *Planning and Using Evaluation Data* (2003), *Managing Evaluation Shortcuts* (2001), and *Mastering ROI* (1998); and *The Human Resources Scorecard: Measuring Return on Investment* (Butterworth-Heinemann, 2001). Phillips can be reached at patti@ roiinstitute.net.

Index

About the American Society for Training & Development

The ASTD Mission: Through exceptional learning and performance, we create a world that works better.

The American Society for Training & Development provides world-class professional development opportunities, content, networking, and resources for workplace learning and performance professionals. Dedicated to helping members increase their relevance, enhance their skills, and align learning to business results, ASTD sets the standard for best practices within the profession.

The society is recognized for shaping global discussions on workforce development and providing the tools to demonstrate the impact of learning on the organizational bottom line. ASTD represents the profession's interests to corporate executives, policy makers, academic leaders, small business owners, and consultants through world-class content, convening opportunities, professional development, and awards and recognition.

Professional Development

> Certificate programs
> Conferences and workshops
> Online learning

> Certified Professional in Learning and Performance (CPLP) certification through the ASTD Certification Institute
> Career Center and Job Bank

Resources

> *T+D* (*Training + Development*) magazine
> ASTD Press
> Industry newsletters
> Research and benchmarking
> Representation to policy makers

Networking

> Local chapters
> Online communities
> ASTD Connect
> Benchmarking Forum
> Learning Executives Network

Awards and Best Practices

> ASTD BEST Awards
> Excellence in Practice Awards
> E-Learning Courseware Certification (ECC) through the ASTD Certification Institute

Learn more about ASTD at www.astd.org.
1.800.628.2783 (U.S.) or 1.703.683.8100
customercare@astd.org

About the ROI Institute

The ROI Institute, Inc. is the leading resource on research, training, and networking for practitioners of the Phillips ROI Methodology.

With a combined 50 years experience in measuring and evaluating training, human resources, technology, and quality programs and initiatives, founders and owners Jack J. Phillips, PhD, and Patti P. Phillips, PhD, are the leading experts in return-on-investment (ROI).

The ROI Institute, founded in 1992, is a service-driven organization that strives to assist professionals in improving their programs and processes through the use of the ROI Methodology. Developed by Jack Phillips, this methodology is a critical tool for measuring and evaluating programs in 18 different applications in more than 40 countries.

The Institute offers a variety of consulting services, learning opportunities, and publications. In addition, it conducts internal research activities for the organization, other enterprises, public sector entities, industries, and interest groups. Together with their team, Jack and Patti Phillips serve private and public sector organizations globally.